French

SPARK PUBLISHING

SPARKNOTES is a registered trademark of SparkNotes LLC

Spark Publishing
A Division of Barnes & Noble Publishing
120 Fifth Avenue
New York, NY 10011
www.sparknotes.com

Please submit all comments and questions or report errors to www.sparknotes.com/errors.

Printed and bound in the United States.

Library of Congress Cataloging-in-Publication Data

Let's Talk French.
     p. cm.
  ISBN-10:1-4114-0443-2
  ISBN-13: 978-1-4114-0443-4
  1. French language—Conversation and phrase books—English.
  2. French language—Textbooks for foreign speakers—English.
PC2121.L545 2006
448.2'421—dc22

                                        2005026101

Contents

Starting from *Bonjour*

1

Greetings

Good morning.
Bonjour.
bon-zhoor.

Good afternoon.
Bonjour.
bon-zhoor.

Good evening.
Bonsoir.
bon-swah.

Hello.
Bonjour. / Salut.
bon-zhoor. / sah-lew

Hi / Hey.
Salut.
sah-lew.

What's up?
Quoi de neuf?
kwah d'nuhf?

Nothing much.
Comme d'habitude.
kuhm dah-bee-tewd.

How are you? / How's it going?
Ça va? / Comment ça va?
sah vah? / kom-mahn sah vah?

Great.
Ça va très bien.
sah vah treh byahn.

Well / fine.
Ça va bien.
sah vah byahn.

Okay.
Ça va.
sah vah.

Not so great.
Ça va pas très fort.
sah vah pah treh for.

I'm really tired.
Je suis très fatigué(e).
zhuh swee treh fah-tee-gay.

I'm hung over.
J'ai la gueule de bois.
zhay la guhl duh bwah.

I'm broke. Can I borrow some [euros]?
Je suis fauché(e). Je peux vous emprunter
(t'emprunter) quelques [euros]?
zhuh swee foh-shay. zhuh puh vooz um-prun-
tay (tum-prun-tay) kel-kuh-[zuhr-oh]?

How is your family?
Comment va votre (ta) famille?
ko-mah vah vohtr (tah) fah-meey?

How are your wife/husband and kids?
Comment va votre (ta) femme / votre (ton) mari
et tes enfants?
ko-mah vah vohtr (tah) fahm / vohtr (ton) mah-ree
ey tay-zahn-fahn?

Great, thanks. And you?
Très bien, merci. Et vous (toi)?
treh byahn, mair-see. ey voo (twah)?

Goodbyes

Goodbye.
Au revoir.
oh re-vwahr.

Bye.
Salut.
sah-LEW.

See you soon.
A bientôt.
ah byahn-toh.

See you later.
A plus tard.
ah plew tar.

See you in the morning.
A demain matin.
ah duh-man mah-tan.

Have a nice day.
Bonne journée.
bun zhoor-nay.

Have a great time.
Amuse-toi bien. (Amusez-vous bien.)
ah-mewz twah byahn. (ah-mew-zay voo byahn.)

Have a nice life.
Bonne vie.
bun vee.

Good night.
Bonne nuit.
bon nwee.

Sleep well.
Dors bien. (Dormez bien.)
dor byahn. (dor-may byahn.)

Sweet dreams.
Fais (Faîtes) de beaux rêves.
fay (fet) duh boh rev.

Introductions

What's your name?
Comment t'appelles-tu? (Comment vous appellez-vous?)
ko-mah tah-pel-tew? (ko-mah voo-zah-play-voo?)

My name is _____.
Je m'appelle _____.
zhuh mah-pel _____.

My friends call me _____.
Mes amis m'appellent _____.
meh-zah-mee mah-pel _____.

Pleased to meet you.
Enchanté(e).
ahn-shahn-tay.

I've heard so much about you.
J'ai beaucoup entendu parlé de toi (de vous).
zhay boh-koo ahn-tahn-dew par-lay duh twah (duh voo).

It was nice to meet you.
J'étais heureux (heureuse) de te (vous) rencontrer.
zhay-tay uhr-uh (uhr-uhz) duh te (voo) rahn-kon-tray.

I love your shoes.
J'aime beaucoup tes (vos) chaussures.
zhem boh-koo tay (voh) shoh-soor.

I'd like you to meet _____.
J'aimerais te présenter (vous présenter) _____.
zhuh-me-ray te pray-zahn-tay (voo pray-zahn-tay) _____.

He / She's my friend.
C'est un ami / C'est une amie à moi.
se-tuhn ah-mee / se-tune ah-mee ah mwa.

He / She's from _____.
Il / Elle vient de _____.
eel / el vyahn duh _____.

He / She's a friend of _____'s.
Il / Elle est un ami / une amie de _____.
eel / el eh-tuhn ah-mee / ewn ah-mee duh _____.

He / She's in town for _____ days.
Il / Elle est ici pour _____ jours.
eel / el eht ee-see poor _____ zhoor.

Do you speak English?
Tu parles anglais? (Vous parlez anglais?)
tew parl ahn-gleh? (voo par-lay ahn-gleh?)

Your English is great!
Tu parles très bien anglais! (Vous parlez très bien anglais!)
tew parl treh byahn ahn-gleh! (voo par-lay treh byahn ahn-gleh!)

I speak only a little [French].
Je ne parle qu'un petit peu de [français].
zhuh ne parl kuhn p-tee puh duh [frahn-se].

Getting Help

Can you help me, please?
Pourriez-vous m'aider s'il vous plaît?
poor-yay voo meh-day seel voo pleh?

Can you do me a favor?
Pourriez-vous (pourrais-tu) me rendre un service?
poor-yay voo (poo-reh tew) me rahndr uhn sair-veess?

Can you spare some change?
Pourriez-vous (pourrais-tu) m'aider avec
un peu de monnaie?
*poor-yay voo (poo-reh tew) meh-day ah-vek
uhn puh duh mo-nay?*

Would you mind ...
Pourriez-vous (Pourrais-tu) ...
poor-yay voo (poo-reh-tew) ...

> **watching my bag?**
> surveiller mon sac?
> *sur-veh-yay mon sahk?*

> **saving my seat ?**
> garder ma place?
> *gar-day mah plahs?*

> **spreading this suntan lotion on my back ?**
> me mettre cette crème solaire dans le dos?
> *me metr set crem so-lair dahn luh doh?*

Pleasantries

Thank you.
Merci.
mair-see.

I really appreciate it.
J'apprécie beaucoup.
zhah-pray-see boh-koo.

You're welcome.
De rien.
duh ryahn.

Don't mention it.
Ce n'est rien. / Je vous en prie. (Je t'en prie.)
se neh ryahn. / zhuh voo-zahn pree. (zhuh tahn pree.)

Excuse me.
Pardon. / Excusez-moi. (Excuse-moi.)
par-DON. / ex-kew-zay mwah. (ex-kewz mwah.)

Sorry.
Je suis désolé(e).
zhuh swee day-zo-lay.

Can you ever forgive me?
Je vous en prie (Je t'en prie) de m'excuser?
zhuh voo-zahn pree (zhuh tahn pree) duh mex-kew-zay?

Asking

who?	qui?	*kee?*
what?	quoi?	*kwah?*
when?	quand?	*kahn?*
where?	où?	*oo?*
why?	pourquoi?	*poor-kwah?*
which?	quel(le)	*kel?*
how?	comment?	*ko-mah?*
how much?	combien?	*kom-byahn?*
how many?	combien de?	*kom-byahn duh?*

Answering

yes.	oui.	*wee.*
no.	non.	*naw.*
maybe.	peut-être.	*puh-tet-r.*

Numbers

0	zéro	*zay-ro*
1	un	*uhn*
2	deux	*duh*
3	trois	*twah*
4	quatre	*kat-r*
5	cinq	*sahnk*
6	six	*seess*
7	sept	*set*
8	huit	*weet*
9	neuf	*nuhf*
10	dix	*deess*
11	onze	*onz*
12	douze	*dooz*
13	treize	*trez*
14	quatorze	*ka-torz*
15	quinze	*kanz*
16	seize	*sez*
17	dix-sept	*deess-set*

STARTING FROM BONJOUR

18	dix-huit	*dee-zweet*
19	dix-neuf	*deez-nuhf*
20	vingt	*vahnt*
21	vingt et un	*vahn-teh uhn*
22	vingt-deux	*vahn-duh*
30	trente	*trahnt*
40	quarante	*ka-rahnt*
50	cinquante	*sang-kahnt*
60	soixante	*swah-sahnt*
70	soixante-dix	*swah-sahnt-deess*
80	quatre-vingt	*kat-ruh-vant*
90	quatre-vingt-dix	*kat-ruh-van-deess*
100	cent	*sahn*
200	deux cents	*duh sahn*
500	cinq cents	*sahnk sanh*
1,000	mille	*meely*
100,000	cent mille	*sahn meely*
1,000,000	un million	*uhn mee-yon*
first	premier (première)	*pre-myay (pre-MYEHR)*
second	deuxième	*duh-zyem*
third	troisième	*trwah-zyem*
fourth	quatrième	*kat-ree-yem*
fifth	cinquième	*sahnk-yem*
sixth	sixième	*see-zyem*
seventh	septième	*set-yem*
eighth	huitième	*weet-yem*

ninth	neuvième	*nuh-vyem*
tenth	dixième	*dee-zyem*
one-half / **a half**	un demi / la moitié	*uhn duh-mee /* *lah mwah-tyay*
one-third / **a third**	un tiers / un troisième	*uhn tyair /* *uhn trwah-zyem*
one-fourth / **a quarter**	un quart	*uhn kar*

How old are you?
Vous avez (Tu as) quel âge?
vooz avay (too ah) kel ahzh?

I'm [23] years old.
J'ai [23] ans.
zhay [van-twaz]ahn.

How much does this cost?
Combien (ça) coûte?
kom-byahn (sah) koot?

It costs [27] euros.
Ça coûte [27] euros.
sah koot [van-set]uhr-oh.

Colors

white	blanc	*blahnk*
pink	rose	*roze*
purple	violet	*vee-oh-lay*
red	rouge	*roozh*
orange	orange	*o-rahnzh*
yellow	jaune	*zhone*

green	vert	*vair*
blue	bleu	*bluh*
brown	marron	*mah-ron*
gray	gris	*gree*
black	noir	*nwar*

Months and Seasons

January	janvier	*zhahn-vyay*
February	février	*fay-vree-yay*
March	mars	*marz*
April	avril	*ahv-reel*
May	mai	*mai*
June	juin	*zhwah*
July	juillet	*zhwee-yay*
August	août	*oot*
September	septembre	*sep-tahm-br*
October	octobre	*ok-toh-br*
November	novembre	*no-vahm-br*
December	décembre	*day-sahm-br*

spring	le printemps	*luh pran-tahm*
summer	l'été	*lay-tay*
fall / autumn	l'automne	*loh-tum*
winter	l'hiver	*lee-vair*

[two] months ago
il y a [deux] mois
eel yah [duh] mwah

last month
le mois dernier
luh mwah der-nyay

this month
ce mois-ci
suh mwah see

next month
le mois prochain
luh mwah pro-shan

in [two] months
dans [deux] mois
dahn [duh] mwah

[two] years ago
il y a [deux] ans
eel yah [duz]ahn

last year
l'année dernière
lah-nay dairn-yare

this year
cette année
set ahn-nay

next year
l'année prochaine
lahn-nay pro-shen

in [two] years
dans [deux] ans
dahn [duhz]ahn

Days and Weeks

Monday	lundi	*luhn-dee*
Tuesday	mardi	*mar-dee*
Wednesday	mercredi	*mair-kre-dee*
Thursday	jeudi	*zhuh-dee*
Friday	vendredi	*vahn-dre-dee*
Saturday	samedi	*sahm-dee*
Sunday	dimanche	*dee-mahnsh*

[three] days ago
il y a [trois] jours
eel yah [trwah] zhoor

the day before yesterday
avant-hier
ah-vahn-tee-yair

yesterday
hier
ee-yair

today
aujourd'hui
oh-zhoor-dwee

tomorrow
demain
duh-man

the day after tomorrow
après-demain
ah-preh-duh-man

in [three] days
dans [trois] jours
dahn [trwah] zhoor

weekend
le week-end
luh wee-kend

last [Monday]
[lundi] dernier
[luhn-dee] der-nyay

this [Monday]
ce [lundi]
suh [luhn-dee]

next [Monday]
[lundi] prochain
[luhn-dee] pro-shan

What day of the week is it?
C'est quel jour de la semaine?
seh kel zhoor duh lah suh-men?

What's today's date?
Quelle est la date aujourd'hui?
kel eh la daht oh-zhoor-dwee?

It's [September 16th].
C'est le [16 septembre].
seh luh [sez sep-tahm-br].

Today is the [16th].
Aujourd'hui, on est le [16].
oh-zhoor-dwee o-neh luh [sez].

[two] weeks ago
il y a [deux] semaines
eel yah [duh] suh-men

last week
la semaine dernière
lah suh-men der-nyear

this week
cette semaine
set suh-men

next week
la semaine prochaine
lah suh-men pro-shen

in [two] weeks
dans [deux] semaines
dahn [duh] suh-men

Telling Time

Excuse me, what time is it?
Excusez-moi (Excuse-moi), il est quelle heure
s'il vous (te) plaît?
*ex-kew-zay-mwah (ex-kewz-mwah), eel eh ke-luhr
seel voo (tuh) pleh?*

It's ...
Il est ...
eel eh ...

> **9:00 [in the morning].**
> neuf heures [du matin].
> *nuh-vuhr [dew mah-tan].*
>
> **noon.**
> midi.
> *mee-dee.*
>
> **3:00 [in the afternoon].**
> trois heures [de l'après-midi].
> *trwah-zuhr [duh lah-preh mee-dee].*
>
> **7:00 [in the evening].**
> sept heures [du soir].
> *set uhr [dew swahr].*

10:00 [at night].
dix heures [du soir].
dee-zuhr [dew swahr].

midnight.
minuit.
mee-nwee.

2:00 [in the morning].
deux heures [du matin].
duh-zuhr [dew mah-tan].

4:00.
quatre heures.
kat-ruhr.

4:10.
quatre heures dix.
kat-ruhr deess.

4:15 (quarter past 4).
quatre heures et quart.
kat-ruhr eh kar.

4:20.
quatre heures vingt.
kat-ruhr van.

4:30 (half past 4).
quatre heures et demi.
kat-ruhr eh duh-mee.

4:45 (quarter to 5).
cinq heures moins le quart.
senk uhr mwah luh kar.

4:50 (ten to 5).
cinq heures moins dix.
senk uhr mwah deess.

morning
le matin
luh mah-tan

day
le jour
luh zhoor

afternoon
l'après-midi
lah-preh mee-dee

evening
le soir / la soirée
luh swahr / la swah-ray

night
la nuit
lah nwee

two nights ago
il y a deux soirs
eel yah duh swahr

last night
hier soir
yair swahr

tonight
ce soir
se swahr

tomorrow night
demain soir
duh-man swahr

the morning after
le lendemain matin
luh lahn-duh-man mah-tan

How long will it take?
Ça prendra combien de temps?
sah prahn-drah kom-byahn duh tahn?

>   **An hour.**
>   Une heure.
>   *ewn uhr.*
>
>   **Two hours.**
>   Deux heures.
>   *duh-zuhr.*
>
>   **Half an hour.**
>   Une demi heure.
>   *ewn duh-mee uhr.*
>
>   **Ten minutes.**
>   Dix minutes.
>   *dee mee-newt.*

before
avant
ah-vahn

after
après
ah-preh

during
pendant
pahn-dahn

[two] hours ago
il y a [deux] heures
eel yah [duhz]uhr

in [two] hours
dans [deux] heures
dahn [duhz]uhr

[two] hours later
[deux] heures plus tard
[duhz]uhr plew tar

[two] hours earlier
[deux] heures plus tôt
[duhz]uhr plew toh

~~~~~~~~~~~~~~~~~~

See you ...
À ...
ah ...

tomorrow morning.
demain matin.
duh-man mah-tan.

[Tuesday] night.
[mardi] soir.
[mar-dee] swahr.

~~~~~~~~~~~~~~~~~~

every day
chaque jour
shahk zhoor

forever
pour toujours
poor too-zhoor

always
toujours
too-zhoor

sometimes
parfois
par-fwah

never
jamais
zhah-meh

Getting There

Tickets

a ... ticket
un billet ...
uhn bee-yay ...

one-way
aller simple
ah-lay sampl

round-trip
aller retour
ah-lay ruh-toor

student
étudiant
ay-tew-dyahn

cheap
pas cher
pah shair

economy / coach class
classe économie / seconde classe
klahs ay-ko-no-mee / sgond klahs

business class
business
beez-nes

first class
première classe
pruh-myear klahs

ticket counter
la billetterie / le comptoir
lah bee-yet-ree / luh kom-twahr

discount
une réduction
ewn ray-dewk-syon

I'd like a one-way ticket to [Paris], please.
J'aimerais un aller simple pour [Paris], s'il vous plaît.
zhem-reh uhn ah-lay sampl poor [pah-ree] seel voo pleh.

I need to ...
Je voudrais ...
zhuh voo-dreh ...

> ### change my ticket.
> changer mon billet.
> *shahn-zhay mon bee-yay.*

> ### return my ticket.
> me faire rembourser mon billet.
> *muh fair rahm-boor-say mon bee-yay.*

I lost my ticket.
J'ai perdu mon billet.
zhay pair-dew mon bee-yay.

I demand a refund.
J'exige un remboursement.
zeh-gzeezh uhn rahm-boors-mahn.

Making Reservations

I'm staying ...
Je suis ...
zhuh swee ...

> **in a hotel.**
> dans un hôtel.
> *dahn-zuhn oh-tel.*

> **at an inn.**
> dans une auberge.
> *dahn-zewn oh-bairzh.*

> **at a bed-and-breakfast.**
> dans une chambre d'hôte.
> *dahn zewn shahm-br dote.*

> **at a hostel.**
> dans une auberge de jeunesse.
> *dahn-zewn oh-bairzh duh zhuh-ness.*

> **at a campsite.**
> dans un camping.
> *dahn-zuhn kahm-peeng.*

> **by the beach.**
> près de la plage.
> *preh duh lah plahzh.*

> **with a friend.**
> avec un/une ami(e).
> *ah-vek uhn [ewn] ah-mee.*

> **with you!**
> avec vous! (avec toi!)
> *ah-vek voo! (ah-vek twah!)*

I'd like to make reservation ...
J'aimerais réserver ...
zhem-ray ray-zair-vay ...

for one night.
pour une nuit.
poor ewn nwee.

for two nights.
pour deux nuits.
poor duh nwee.

for three nights.
pour trois nuits.
poor trwah nwee.

for a week.
pour une semaine.
poor ewn suh-men.

for one person.
pour une personne.
poor ewn pair-suhn.

for two people.
pour deux personnes.
poor duh pair-suhn.

for two girls.
pour deux filles.
poor duh feey.

for two guys.
pour deux garçons.
poor duh gar-son.

for a couple.
pour un couple.
poor uhn koop-l.

Do you take credit cards?
Vous accepter les cartes de crédit?
voo-zahk-sep-tay lay kart duh kray-dee?

How much is ...
Combien coûte ...
kom-byahn koot ...

a room?
une chambre?
ewn shahm-br?

a single room?
une chambre simple?
ewn shahm-br sampl?

a double room...
une chambre double...
ewn shahm-br doobl...

with a shower?
avec douche?
ah-vek doosh?

with a bathtub?
avec baignoire / bain?
ah-vek beng-wahr / ban?

with a sink?
avec évier?
ah-vek ay-vyay?

with a toilet?
avec toilettes?
ah-vek twah-let?

with a TV?
avec une télé?
ah-vek ewn tay-lay?

with a refrigerator?
avec un frigo?
ah-vek uhn free-goh?

with air conditioning?
avec de la climatisation?
ah-vek duh lah klee-mah-tee-zah-syon?

a private room?
une chambre privé?
ewn shahm-br pree-vay?

a shared room?
une chambre à partager?
ewn shahm-br ah par-tah-zhay?

a bunk bed?
une chambre avec un lit superposé?
ewn shahm-br ah-vek uhn lee sew-pair-poh-say?

an extra bed?
un lit en plus?
uhn lee ahn plewss?

male	homme	*um*
female	femme	*fahm*
single-sex	uni-sexe	*ew-nee-sex*
co-ed	mixte	*meext*

Do you provide ...
Vous fournissez ...
voo foor-nee-say ...

bedding?
de la literie?
duh lah leet-ree?

sheets?
des draps?
day drah?

towels?
des serviettes?
day sair-vyet?

toiletries?
des articles de toilette?
de-zar-teekl duh twah-let?

a mini-bar?
un mini-bar ?
uhn mee-nee-bar?

Is there ...
Est-ce qu'il y a ...
es keel yah ...

a pool?	une piscine?	*ewn pee-seen?*
a gym?	une salle de sport?	*ewn sahl duh spor?*
a kitchen?	une cuisine?	*ewn kwee-zeen?*

What time is ...
A quelle heure est ...
ah kel uhr eh ...

check-in?	l'enregistre-ment?	*lahn-re-zhees-tr-mahn?*
checkout?	le départ?	*luh day-par?*

Can I leave my luggage for the day?
Je peux laisser mes bagages pour la journée?
zhuh puh leh-say meh bah-gazh poor lah zhoor-nay?

Do I need my own lock?
J'ai besoin d'un cadenas?
zhay be-zwahn duhn kah-d-nah?

Please give me directions ...
Est-ce que vous pourriez me donnez des indications ...
es kuh voo poor-yay muh do-nay de-zahn-dee-kah-syon ...

> **from the airport.**
> depuis l'aéroport, s'il vous plaît.
> *duh-pwee lair-ro-por, seel voo pleh.*

> **from the train station.**
> depuis la gare, s'il vous plaît.
> *duh-pwee lah gar, seel voo pleh.*

> **from the bus station.**
> depuis la station de bus, s'il vous plaît.
> *duh-pwee lah stah-syon duh bewss, seel voo pleh.*

In Transit

I'm traveling ...
Je voyage ...
zhuh vwah-yazh ...

> **by airplane.**
> en avion.
> *ahn ah-vyon.*

> **by train / rail.**
> en train.
> *ahn tran.*

> **by subway.**
> en métro.
> *ahn may-tro.*

by bus / coach.
en bus.
ahn bewss.

by car.
en voiture.
ahn vwah-ture.

by taxi.
en taxi.
ahn tah-ksee.

by bicycle.
en vélo.
ahn vay-lo.

on horseback.
à cheval.
ah she-vahl.

on foot.
à pied.
ah pyeh.

2

GETTING THERE

with friends.
avec des amis.
ah-vek day-zah-mee.

with my parents.
avec mes parents.
ah-vek meh pah-rahn.

with my entourage.
avec ma bande.
ah-vek mah bahnd.

alone.
seul(e).
suhl.

Air Travel

flight
vol
vol

airport
aéroport
air-ro-por

airline
compagnie aérienne
kom-pah-nyee air-yen

connection
connexion
ko-nek-syon

layover
changement
shahn-zh-mahn

delay
retard
ruh-tar

ticket
billet
bee-yay

pilot
pilote
pee-lut

flight attendant
steward / personnel naviguant
stew-wahr / pair-so-nel nah-vee-gahn

Where is / are the ...
Où est / Où sont ...
oo eh / oo son ...

check-in counter?
le comptoir d'enregistrement?
luh kon-twahr dahn-re-zhees-tr-mahn?

departures?
les départs?
lay day-par?

arrivals?
les arrivées?
lay-zah-ree-vay?

gate?
la porte?
lah port?

baggage claim?
le carrousel?
luh ka-roo-zel?

lost-and-found?
les objets perdus?
lay-zob-zhay pair-dew?

bar?
le bar?
luh bar?

I'm on flight [101] to [Marseilles].
Je suis sur le vol [101] pour [Marseilles].
zhuh swee sur luh vol [sahn-t uhn] poor [mar-sey].

What time does the flight to [Lyon] leave?
Le vol pour [Lyon] part à quelle heure?
luh vol poor [lyon] par ah kel uhr?

Which gate does it leave from?
Ce vol part de quelle porte?
suh vol par duh kel port?

I need to check two bags.
J'ai deux bagages à enregistrer.
zhay duh bah-gazh ah ahn-re-zhees-tray.

I only have carry-on luggage.
Je n'ai qu'un sac de cabine.
zhuh nay kuhn sahk duh kah-been.

I need a boarding pass.
J'ai besoin d'une carte d'embarquement.
zhay be-zwahn dewn kart dahm-bark-mahn.

~~~

Is the flight ...
Est-ce que le vol est ...
es kuh luh vol eh ...

on time?	à l'heure?	*ah luhr?*
early?	en avance?	*ah-nah-vahns?*
late?	en retard?	*ahn ruh-tar?*
delayed?	retardé?	*ruh-tar-day?*
canceled?	annulé?	*ah-new-lay?*

~~~

I'm in ...
Je suis ...
zhuh swee ...

first class.
en première classe.
ahn pre-myehr klahs.

business class.
en business classe.
ahn beez-ness klahs.

economy / coach.
en classe économie.
ahn klahs ay-ko-no-mee.

an aisle seat.
dans l'allée.
dahn lah-lay.

a window seat.
à une place avec hublot.
ah ewn plahs ah-vek ewb-loh.

the bathroom.
aux toilettes.
oh twah-let.

My luggage is ...
Mes bagages sont ...
meh bah-gahzh son ...

missing.
perdus.
pair-dew.

damaged.
abîmés. / endommagés.
ah-bee-may. / ahn-do-mah-zhay.

really heavy.
très lourds.
treh loor.

Train Travel

train
train
tran

tracks
voies
vwah

baggage locker
casier
kah-zyay

compartment
compartiment
kom-par-tee-mahn

dining car
wagon-bar / wagon-restaurant
vah-gon bar / vah-gon res-to-rahn

Where is the train station?
Où est la gare?
oo eh lah gar?

I'm on the [5:00] train to [Toulouse].
Je suis dans le train de [17h] pour [Toulouse].
zhuh swee dahn luh trahn duh [deess-set uhr] poor [too-looz].

What time does the train to [Nice] leave?
Le train pour [Nice] part à quelle heure?
luh tran poor [neess] par ah kel uhr?

Which platform does it leave from?
De quelle voie?
duh kel vwah?

I'd like a ticket ...

J'aimerais un billet ...

zhem-reh uhn bee-yeh ...

in the smoking section.

fumeur.

foo-mur.

in the nonsmoking section.

non fumeur.

non foo-mur.

on the overnight train.

pour le train de nuit.

poor luh tran duh nwee.

in the sleeping car.

en couchette.

ahn koo-shet.

I need ...

J'ai besoin ...

zhay be-zwahn ...

some sheets.

des draps.

day drah.

a blanket.

d'une couverture.

dewn koo-vair-ture.

some pillows.

d'oreillers.

do-reh-yay.

Bus Travel

Where is the bus station?
Où est la station de bus?
oo eh lah stah-syon duh bewss?

Do I need a reservation?
Est-ce que je dois réserver?
es kuh zhuh dwah ray-zair-vay?

Can you turn up the heat, please?
Est-ce que vous pouvez monter le chauffage,
s'il vous plaît?
es kuh voo poo-vay mon-tay luh shoh-fahzh
see voo pleh?

Can you turn down the heat, please?
Est-ce que vous pouvez baisser le chauffage,
s'il vous plaît?
es kuh voo poo-vay bess-say luh shoh-fahzh,
see voo pleh?

How much longer?
Il reste encore combien de temps?
eel rest anh-kor kom-byahn duh tahn?

Are we there yet?
On est arrivé?
on et ah-ree-vay?

Passport and Customs

passport
passeport
pahs-por

visa
visa
vee-zah

ID
pièce d'identité
pyes dee-dahn-tee-tay

driver's license
permit de conduire
pair-mee duh kon-dweer

customs
douane
dwahn

declaration form
déclaration
dey-klah-rah-syon

~~~~~~~~~~~~~~~~~~~~~~~~~~~~~~~~~~~

I'm traveling on business.
Je suis en voyages d'affaires.
zhuh sweez on vwah-yahzh dah-fair.

I'm traveling for pleasure.
Je voyage pour le plaisir.
zhuh vwah-yazh poor luh play-zeer.

~~~~~~~~~~~~~~~~~~~~~~~~~~~~~~~~~~~

I'm an [American] citizen.
Je suis un citoyen [américain].
zhuh swee uhn see-twah-yahn [ah-meh-ree-kan].

I lost my passport.
J'ai perdu mon passeport.
zhay pair-dew mon pahs-por.

I plan to stay ...
Je compte rester ...
zhuh kont res-tay ...

for [three] days.
[trois] jours.
[trwah] zhoor.

for [one] month.
[un] mois.
[uhn] mwah.

until I find what I'm looking for.
jusqu'à ce que je trouve ce que je cherche.
zhuce-kahs kuh zhuh troov suh kuh zhuh shairsh.

until I clear my name.
jusqu'à ce que je clarifie ma situation.
zhuce-kahs kuh zhuh klah-ree-fee mah see-tew-ah-syon.

forever.
pour toujours.
poor too-zhoor.

I'm only passing through.
Je suis de passage.
zhuh swee duh pah-sazh.

I have nothing to declare.
Je n'ai rien à déclarer.
zhuh nay ryahn ah day-klah-ray.

Countries and Nationalities

England / English
Angleterre / anglais(e)
ahn-gluh-tai / ahn-gleh (ang-glez)

France / French
France / français(e)
frahns / frahn-seh (frahn-sez)

Spain / Spanish
Espagne / espagnol(e)
es-pah-nyuh / es-pah-nyol

Portugal / Portuguese
Portugal / portugais(e)
por-tew-gahl / por-tew-geh (por-tew-gez)

Italy / Italian
Italie / italien(ne)
ee-tah-lee / ee-tah-lyahn (ee-tah-lyen)

Greece / Greek
Grèce / grec (grecque)
gress / grek

Germany / German
Allemagne / allemand(e)
ahl-mah-nyuh / ahl-mahn (ahl-mahnd)

Russia / Russian
Russie / russe
rew-see / rewss

United States / American
Etats-Unis / américain(e)
ay-tah-zew-nee / ah-meh-ree-kan (ah-meh-ree-ken)

Canada / Canadian
Canada / canadien(ne)
kah-nah-dah / kah-nah-dyahn (kah-nah-dyen)

Mexico / Mexico
Mexique / mexicain(e)
meh-kseek / meh-ksee-kan (meh-ksee-ken)

Brazil / Brazilian
Brésil / brésilien(ne)
bray-zeel / bray-zee-lyahn (bray-zee-lyen)

Argentina / Argentine
Argentine / argentin(e)
ar-zhahn-teen / ar-zhahn-tan (ar-zhahn-teen)

Morocco / Moroccan
Maroc / marocain(e)
mah-rok / mah-ro-kan (mah-ro-ken)

Egypt / Egyptian
Egypte / égyptien(ne)
ay-zheept / ay-zheep-tyahn (ay-zheep-tyen)

Israel / Israeli
Israël / israélien(ne)
ees-rah-yel / ees-rah-lyahn (ees-rah-eh-lyen)

China / Chinese
Chine / chinois(e)
sheen / shee-nwah (shee-nwahz)

India / Indian
Inde / indien(ne)
ahnd / ahn-dyahn (ahn-dyen)

Korea / Korean
Corée / coréen(ne)
ko-ray / ko-ray-ahn (ko-ray-en)

Japan / Japanese
Japon / japonais(e)
zhah-pon / zhah-po-neh (zha-po-nez)

Thailand / Thai
Thaïlande / thaïlandais(e)
tie-lahnd / tie-lahn-deh (tie-lahn-dez)

Australia / Australian
Australie / australien(ne)
ohs-trah-lee / ohs-trah-lyahn (ohs-trah-lyen)

New Zealand / Kiwi
Nouvelle Zélande / néo-zélandais(e)
noo-vel zay-lahnd / nay-oh-zay-lahn-deh (nay-oh-zay-lahn-dez)

Checking In

reception
accueil / réception
ahk-koy / ray-sep-syon

check-in
enregistrement
ahn-re-zhees-truh-mahn

check-out
règlement / départ
reg-luh-mahn / day-par

deposit
caution
koh-syon

key
clé
klay

keycard
carte électronique
kart ay-lek-tro-neek

Do I need a reservation?
Est-ce que j'ai besoin de réserver?
es kuh zhay be-zwahn duh ray-zair-vay?

I'd like to check in.
J'aimerais me faire enregistrer.
zhem-reh muh fair ahn-re-zhees-tray.

I have a reservation for tonight.
J'ai réservé pour ce soir.
zhay ray-zair-vay poor suh swahr.

Can I change my reservation?
Est-ce que je peux changer ma réservation?
es kuh zhuh puh shahn-zhay mah ray-zair-vah-syon?

I'd like to cancel my reservation.
J'aimerais annuler ma réservation.
zhem-reh ahn-new-lay mah ray-zair-vah-syon.

Is there an elevator?
Est-ce qu'il y a un ascenseur?
es keel yah uhn ah-sahn-suhr?

Can you please help me with my luggage?
Pourriez-vous m'aider avec mes bagages,
s'il vous plaît?
poor-yay voo meh-day ah-vek meh bah-gazh, see voo pleh?

Can I have an extra key?
Est-ce que je pourrais avoir une clé
supplémentaire?
*es kuh zhuh poo-reh ah-vwahr ewn klay
sew-play-mahn-tare?*

Here is your tip. Thanks.
Voilà votre pourboire. Merci.
vwah-lah votr poor-bwahr. mair-see.

My room is ...
Ma chambre est ...
mah shahm-br eh ...

too small.
trop petite.
troh puh-teet.

too dirty.
trop sale.
troh sahl.

too hot.
trop chaude.
troh shode.

too cold.
trop froide.
troh frwahd.

just right.
très bien.
treh byahn.

perfect.
parfaite.
par-fet.

crawling with ants.
pleine de fourmis.
plen duh foor-mee.

I need new sheets.
J'ai besoin de nouveaux draps.
zhay be-zwahn duh noo-voh drah.

The ... doesn't work.
... ne marche pas.
... nuh marsh pah.

   light switch
   la lumière
   lah lew-myear

   alarm clock
   le réveil
   luh ray-vey

TV
la télé
lah tay-lay

sink
l'évier
lay-vyay

shower
la douche
lah doosh

refrigerator
le frigo
luh free-goh

air conditioning
la climatisation
lah klee-mah-tee-zah-syon

heat
le chauffage
luh shoh-fahzh

The toilet doesn't work.
Les toilettes ne marchent pas.
lay twah-let nuh mar-shahn pas.

What is the phone number here?
Quel est le numéro de téléphone ici?
kel eh luh new-may-roh duh tay-lay-fun ee-see?

Are there any messages for me?
Il y a des messages pour moi?
eel yah day meh-sazh poor mwah?

I'm in room [212].
Je suis dans la chambre [212].
zhuh swee dahn lah shahm-br [duh sahn dooz].

I lost the key to my room.
J'ai perdu la clé de ma chambre.
zhay pair-dew lah klay duh mah shahm-br.

What time is breakfast?
Le petit déjeuner est à quelle heure?
luh puh-tee day-zhuh-nay eh-t ah kel uhr?

Is there someone here all night?
Est-ce qu'il y a quelqu'un ici toute la nuit?
es keel yah kel-kun ee-see toot lah nwee?

How late can I stay out?
Je peux rester dehors jusqu'à quelle heure?
zhuh puh res-tay duh-or zhews-kah kel uhr?

I need a wake-up call.
J'ai besoin d'un réveille téléphonique.
zhay be-zwahn duhn ray-vey tay-lay-fo-neek.

Let me in!
Laissez-moi entrer!
leh-say mwah ahn-tray!

Relief!

toilet
toilettes
twah-let

sink
évier
ay-vyay

toilet paper
papier hygiénique / PQ
pahp-yay ee-zheh-neek / pay-koo

Where's the ...
Où sont les ...
oo son lay ...

bathroom?
toilettes?
twah-let?

ladies' room?
toilettes pour femmes?
twah-let poor fahm?

men's room ?
toilettes pour hommes?
twah-let poo-rum?

3

SETTLING IN

It's not working.
Ça ne marche pas.
sah nuh marsh pah.

It won't flush.
La chasse d'eau ne marche pas.
lah shahs doh nuh marsh pah.

It's dirty.
C'est sale.
seh sahl.

It's overflowing.
Ça déborde.
sah day-bord.

Orientation

north	nord	*nor*
south	sud	*sude*
east	est	*est*
west	ouest	*west*

city map
plan de la ville
plahn duh la veel

I'm lost.
Je suis perdu(e).
zhuh swee pair-dew.

Can you tell me where the ... is?
S'il vous plaît, où se trouve le/la ... ?
seel voo pleh, oo s-troov luh/lah ... ?

Where is ...
Où est ...
oo eh ...

> **the tourist office?**
> l'office de tourisme?
> *lo-feess duh too-reezm?*

> **the nearest restaurant?**
> le restaurant le plus proche?
> *luh res-toh-rahn luh plew prosh?*

> **the post office?**
> la poste?
> *lah post?*

> **the police station?**
> le poste de police?
> *luh post duh po-leess?*

> **the center of town?**
> le centre-ville?
> *luh sahn-tr veel?*

Can you tell me how to get there?
Comment je fais pour y aller?
ko-mahn zhuh feh poor ee ah-lay?

Which way do I go?
Je dois aller dans quelle direction?
zhuh dwah-z ah-lay dahn kel dee-rek-syon?

Turn ...
Tournez ...
toor-nay ...

left ...
à gauche ...
ah gohsh ...

right ...
à droite ...
ah drwaht ...

at the corner.
au coin.
oh kwahn.

at the next street.
à la prochaine rue.
ah lah pro-shen rew.

Go straight ahead ...
Aller tout droit ...
ah-lay too drwah ...

down this street.
au bout de la rue.
oh boo duh lah rew.

through the intersection.
et traversez le carrefour.
eh trah-vair-say luh kar-foor.

Am I going the right way?
Est-ce que je vais dans la bonne direction?
es kuh zhuh veh dahn lah bun dee-rek-syon?

SETTLING IN

You're going the wrong way.
Vous allez dans la mauvaise direction.
voo-zah-lay dahn lah moh-vez dee-rek-syon.

Do you have a map?
Est-ce que vous avez (tu as) un plan?
es kuh voo-zavay (tew ah) uhn plahn?

~~~~~~

Can you recommend ...
Vous pouvez (Tu peux) me recommander ...
voo poo-vay (tew puh) muh ruh-ko-mahn-day ...

a place to eat?
un endroit pour manger?
uhn ahn-drwah poor mahn-zhay?

a place to sleep?
un endroit pour dormir?
uhn ahn-drwah poor dor-meer?

a trendy café?
un café branché? / à la mode?
uhn kah-fay brawn-shay? / ah lah mode?

a restaurant that's always open?
un restaurant qui est toujours ouvert?
uhn res-toh-rahn kee eh too-zhoor oo-vair?

a bar?
un bar?
uhn bar?

a dance club? / disco?
une boîte de nuit? / un club?
ewn bwaht duh nwee? / uhn klube?

Local Transportation

Where's the nearest bus stop?
Où est l'arrêt de bus le plus proche?
oo eh lah-reh duh bewss luh plew prosh?

Where can I catch the bus to [Montparnasse]?
Où est-ce que je peux prendre le bus pour [Montparnasse] ?
oo es kuh zhuh puh prahn-dr luh bewss poor [mon-par-nahs]?

Do you stop at [the museum]?
Est-ce que vous vous arrêtez [au musée]?
es kuh voo voo-zah-reh-tay [oh mew-zay] ?

Do you have a bus map?
Auriez-vous un plan de bus?
oh-ryay voo uhn plahn duh bewss?

What's the fare?
Combien ça coûte?
kom-byahn sah koot?

Where's the nearest subway stop?
Où est l'arrêt de métro le plus proche?
oo eh lah-reh duh may-tro luh plew prosh?

I need ...
J'ai besoin ...
zhay be-zwahn ...

> **a ticket. / token.**
> d'un ticket.
> *duhn tee-kay.*

a day pass.
d'un passe pour la journée.
duhn pahss poor lah zhoor-nay.

a weekly pass.
d'un coupon. / d'un passe hebdomadaire.
duhn koo-pon. / duhn pahss eb-do-mah-dare.

---

subway map
plan du métro
plahn dew may-tro

transfer
changement
shahn-zh-mahn

the [red / A / 7] line
la ligne (rouge/ A / 7)
lah lee-nyuh [roozh / ah / set]

Where do I get off?
Je descends où?
zhuh duh-sahn-doo?

At the first stop.
Au premier arrêt.
oh pruh-myay ah-reh.

At the second stop.
Au deuxième arrêt.
au duh-zyem ah-reh.

Where can I catch a taxi?
Où est-ce que je peux trouver un taxi?
oo es kuh zhuh puh troo-vay uhn tah-ksee?

How much is a taxi to [the Louvre]?
Combien coûte un taxi pour aller [au Louvre]?
kom-byahn koot uhn tah-ksee poor ah-lay [oh loovr]?

What's the fare?
Quel est le tarif?
kel eh luh tah-reef?

Please turn the meter on.
Vous pouvez mettre le comptoir s'il vous plaît?
voo poo-vay metr luh kon-twahr see voo pleh?

That's too much.
C'est trop (cher).
seh troh (shair).

4 Wining and Dining

I'm hungry.
J'ai faim.
zhay fahn.

I'm thirsty.
J'ai soif.
zhay swahf.

I'm starving.
Je meurs de faim.
zhuh muhr duh fahn.

I need to eat.
J'ai besoin de manger.
zhay be-zwahn duh mahn-zhay.

I could eat a horse.
J'ai une faim de loup.
zhay ewn fahn duh loo.

I need a drink.
Il me faut un verre.
eel muh foh uhn vair.

I need [several] drinks.
Il me faut [plusieurs] verres.
eel muh foh [plew-zyur] vair.

Meals

breakfast	le petit déjeuner	*luh puh-tee day-zhuh-nay*
lunch	le déjeuner	*luh day-zhuh-nay*
dinner	le dîner	*luh dee-nay*
snack	le goûter	*luh goo-tay*

Courses

salad	salade	*sah-lahd*
appetizer	entrée	*ahn-tray*
main dish / main course	plat	*plah*
side dish	accompagnement	*ahk-kom-pah-nyuh-mahn*
dessert	dessert	*deh-sair*

Utensils

fork	fourchette	*foor-shet*
knife	couteau	*koo-toh*
spoon	cuillère	*kwee-year*
plate	assiette	*ahs-syet*
bowl	bol	*bawl*
cup	tasse	*tahss*
glass	verre	*vair*

Going Out to Eat

Can you recommend a ...
Est-ce que vous pourriez (tu pourrais)
recommander un ...
es kuh voo poor-yay (tew poo-reh) reh-ko-mahn-day uhn ...

restaurant?	restaurant?	*res-toh-rahn?*
bar?	bar?	*bar?*
café?	café?	*kah-fay?*

Is it expensive?
C'est cher?
seh shair?

Is it nearby?
C'est près d'ici?
seh preh dee-see?

What kind of food do they serve?
Ils font quelle sorte de cuisine?
eel fon kel sort duh kwee-zeen?

Do they have vegetarian food?
Ils font de la cuisine végétarienne?
eel fon duh lah kwee-zeen vay-zhay-tah-ryen?

Can they take a big group?
Ils accepteraient un grand groupe?
eel ahk-sep-tuh-ray uhn grahn groop?

Will we need reservations?
Est-ce qu'il faut réserver?
es keel foh ray-zair-vay?

How late do they serve food?
Ils servent à manger jusqu'à quelle heure?
eel sairv ah mahn-zhay zhews-kah kel uhr?

We're in a hurry.
Nous sommes pressé(e)s.
noo sum pruh-say.

We'd like a table for [four].
Nous voudrions une table pour [quatre].
noo voo-dree-on ewn tah-bl poor [katr].

How long is the wait?
Nous devons attendre combien de temps?
noo duh-von ah-tahn-dr kom-byahn duh tahn?

We have a reservation.
Nous avons réservé.
noo-zah-von ray-zair-vay.

The name is ...
Le nom est ...
luh nohn eh ...

We'd like the smoking / non-smoking section.
Nous voudrions le coin fumeur / non-fumeur.
noo voo-dree-on luh kwahn few-moor / non few-moor.

My friends will be here ...
Mes amis seront là ...
meh-zah-mee suh-ron lah ...

> #### soon.
> bientôt.
> *byahn-toh.*
>
> #### in [ten] minutes.
> dans [dix] minutes.
> *dahn [dee] mee-newt.*
>
> #### later.
> plus tard.
> *plew tar.*

Where's the restroom?
Où sont les toilettes, s'il vous plaît?
oo son lay twah-let, see voo pleh?

May I see a menu, please?
Je pourrais voir une carte, s'il vous plaît?
zhuh poo-reh vwahr ewn kart, see voo pleh?

What do you recommend?
Qu'est ce que vous me conseiller?
kess kuh voo muh kon-se-yey?

Do you have any specials?
Est-ce que vous avez des plats du jour?
es kuh voo-zah-vay day plah dew zhoor?

Do you have a kids' menu?
Est-ce que vous avez une carte pour enfants?
es kuh voo-zah-vay ewn kart poor ahn-fahn?

I'm a vegetarian.
Je suis végétarien(ne).
zhuh swee vay-zhay-tah-ryahn (vay-zhay-tah-ryen).

I'll have ...
Je prendrai ...
zhuh prahn-dray ...

He / She will have ...
Il / Elle prendra ...
eel / el prahn-drah ...

I'll have what he/she's having.
Je voudrais la même chose.
zhuh voo-dreh lah mem shoze.

We'd like to split [an appetizer].
Nous voudrions partager [une entrée].
noo voo-dree-on par-tah-zhay [ewn ahn-tray].

Can you hold the [onions]?
C'est possible de l'avoir sans [oignons], s'il vous plaît?
seh po-seebl duh lah-vwahr sahn[-zo-nyon] see voo pleh?

Can I have the [sauce] on the side?
Est-ce que je pourrais avoir [la sauce] à part?
es kuh zhuh poo-reh ah-vwahr [lah sohs] ah par?

~~~

I'd like it ...
Je le voudrais ...
zhuh luh voo-dreh ...

rare.	saignant.	*seh-nyahn.*
medium.	à point.	*ah pwahn.*
well done.	bien cuit.	*byahn kwee.*

~~~

How is everything?
Tout va bien?
too vah byahn?

Everything's great, thank you.
C'est très bien, merci.
seh treh byahn, mair-see.

~~~

It's ...
C'est ...
seh ...

delicious.	délicieux.	*day-lee-syuh.*
bitter.	amer.	*ah-mair.*
sour.	acide.	*ah-seed.*
sweet.	sucré.	*sew-kray.*
hot / spicy.	épicé.	*ay-pee-say.*

the best [artichoke] I've ever had.
le meilleur [artichaut] que j'ai jamais goûté.
luh meh-yoor [ar-tee-shoh] kuh zhay zhah-meh goo-tay.

This is [a little] ...
C'est [un peu] ...
seh [tuhn puh] ...

cold.	froid.	*frwah.*
overcooked.	trop cuit.	*troh kwee.*
burnt.	brûlé.	*brew-lay.*
too salty.	trop salé.	*troh sah-lay.*
rotten.	pourri.	*poo-ree.*

This isn't fresh.
Ce n'est pas frais.
seh neh pah freh.

This is a little undercooked.
Ce n'est pas assez cuit.
seh neh pah ah-say kwee.

Can I have a new [napkin] please?
Est-ce que je pourrais avoir une autre
[serviette] s'il vous plaît?
*es kuh zhuh poo-reh ah-vwahr ewn ohtr
[sair-vyet] seel voo pleh?*

This [fork] is dirty.
Cette [fourchette] est sale.
set / suh [foor-shet] eh sahl.

I'll have another.
Un autre s'il vous plaît.
uhn ohtr seel voo pleh.

I'm full.
Je suis rassasié.
zhuh swee rah-sah-zyay.

I'm stuffed.
Je n'en peux plus.
zhuh nahn puh plew.

I'm still hungry.
J'ai encore faim.
zhay ahn-kor fahn.

Can I take the rest to go?
Est-ce que je peux prendre le reste à emporter, s'il vous plaît?
es kuh zhuh puh prahndr luh rest ah ahm-por-tay, seel voo pleh?

The check, please.
L'addition, s'il vous plaît.
lah-dee-syon, see voo pleh.

Is tip/service included?
Est-ce que le service est compris?
es kuh luh sair-veess eh kom-pree?

I don't think the bill is right.
Je crois qu'il y a un erreur.
zhuh krwah keel yah uhn air-rur.

Do you take credit cards?
Vous acceptez les cartes de crédit?
voo-zahk-sep-tay lay kart duh kray-dee?

Can I get a receipt?
Est-ce que je pourrais avoir un reçu, s'il vous plaît?
es kuh zhuh poo-reh ah-vwahr uhn ruh-sew, see voo pleh?

Preparation

raw	cru(e)	*krew*
fresh	frais (fraîche)	*freh (fresh)*
baked	cuit(e) au four	*kwee-toh foor*
fried	frit(e)	*free (freet)*
roasted	rôti(e)	*roh-tee*

grilled / broiled	grillé(e)	*gree-yay*
sautéed	sauté(e)	*soh-tay*
charred	cuit(e) au gril	*kwee-toh greel*

Foods

meat	viande	*vyahnd*
beef	bœuf	*buhf*
ham	jambon	*zhahm-bon*
pork	porc	*por*
lamb	agneau	*ah-nyoh*
poultry	volaille	*vo-lai*
chicken	poulet	*poo-leh*
turkey	dinde	*dahnd*

fish	poisson	*pwah-son*
salmon	saumon	*soh-mon*
tuna	thon	*ton*
bass	bar	*bar*
shrimp	crevettes	*kreh-vet*
squid	calamars	*kah-lah-mar*

fruits	fruits	*frwee*
apple	pomme	*pum*
orange	orange	*aw-rahnzh*

banana	banane	*bah-nahn*
straw-berry	fraise	*frez*
cherry	cerise	*suh-reez*
grapes	raisins	*reh-zahn*

vegetables / grains	légumes / céréales	*lay-gewm / say-ray-ahl*
potato	pomme de terre	*pum duh tare*
tomato	tomate	*to-maht*
eggplant	aubergine	*oh-bear-zheen*
cucumber	concombre	*kon-kombr*
pepper	poivron	*pwahv-ron*
carrots	carottes	*kah-rot*
onion	oignon	*aw-nyon*
garlic	ail	*aye*
mush-room	champignon	*shahm-pee-nyon*
peas	petits pois	*puh-tee pwah*
corn	maïs	*mah-yeess*
rice	riz	*ree*
beans	légumes secs	*lay-gewm sek*

drinks	boissons	*bwah-sohn*
wine	vin	*vahn*

beer	bière	*byear*
liquor	alcool	*ahl-kuhl*
soda / pop / Coke	soda	*soh-DAH*
water	eau	*oh*
still water	eau plate	*oh plaht*
carbonated	eau gazeuse	*oh gah-zooz*
coffee	café	*kah-fay*
tea	thé	*tay*
milk	lait	*lay*
juice	jus	*zhew*

~~~~~~

spices	épices	*ay-peess*
sugar	sucre	*sewkr*
salt	sel	*sel*
pepper	poivre	*pwahvr*

~~~~~~

desserts	desserts	*de-sair*
cake	gâteau	*gah-toh*
cookie	cookie	*koo-KEE*
torte	tarte	*tart*
cheese	fromage	*fro-mahzh*

I don't eat ...
Je ne mange pas ...
zhuh nuh mahnzh pah ...

red meat. de viande rouge. *uh vyahnd roozh.*

pork. de porc. *duh por.*

fish. de poisson. *duh pwah-son.*

I'm allergic ...
Je suis allergique ...
zhuh swee-zah-lair-zheek ...

to nuts.
aux noix.
oh nwah.

to chocolate.
au chocolat.
oh sho-ko-lah.

to dairy products.
aux produits laitiers.
oh pro-dwee leh-tyay.

I keep kosher.
Je mange casher.
zhuh mahn-zh kah-share.

I'm vegan.
Je suis végétalien.
zhuh swee vay-zhay-tah-lyahn.

I'm Mormon.
Je suis mormon.
zhuh swee mor-mon.

4

Grooming and Primping

Clothes

What are you wearing?
Vous vous habillez (Tu t'habilles) comment?
voo voo zah-bee-yay (tew tah-beey) kom-mah?

I'm wearing ...
Je porte ...
zhuh port ...

a T-shirt.
un T-shirt.
uhn tee-shurt.

a [red] T-shirt.
un T-shirt [rouge].
uhn tee-shurt [roozh].

a short-sleeve shirt.
une chemise à manches courtes.
ewn shuh-meez ah mahnsh koort.

a long-sleeve shirt.
une chemise à manches longues.
ewn shu-meez ah mahnsh lohng.

a sweatshirt.
un sweat.
uhn swet.

a sweater.
un pull.
uhn pewl.

shorts.
un short.
uhn short.

pants .
un pantalon.
uhn pahn-tah-lon.

jeans.
un jean.
uhn jeen.

a belt.
une ceinture.
ewn san-ture.

a skirt.
une jupe.
ewn zhewp.

a dress.
une robe.
ewn robe.

a coat.
un manteau.
uhn mahn-toh.

a jacket.
une veste.
ewn vest.

a tanktop.
un débardeur.
uhn day-bar-dur.

a bra.
un soutien-gorge.
uhn soo-tyahn-gorzh.

a swimsuit.
un maillot.
uhn my-yoh.

a bikini.
un bikini.
uhn bee-kee-NEE.

a hat.
un chapeau.
uhn shah-poh.

underwear.
un sous-vêtement .
uhn soo vet-mahn.

tights.
des bas.
day bah.

nylons.
des bas nylons.
day bah nee-lohn.

shoes.
des chaussures.
day shoh-sewr.

sneakers.
des baskets.
day bahs-ket.

sandals.
des sandales.
day sahn-dahl.

boots.
des bottes.
day bot.

flats.
des chaussures sans talon.
day shoh-sewr sahn tah-lon.

high heels.
des talons-hauts.
day tah-lon-oh.

Cleaning Up

I need to ...
J'ai besoin de ...
zhay be-zwahn duh ...

> **take a shower.**
> prendre une douche.
> *prahndr ewn doosh.*

> **take a bath.**
> prendre un bain.
> *prahndr uhn ban.*

towel	serviette	*sair-vyet*
soap	savon	*sah-von*
shampoo	shampooing	*shahm-po-ing*
conditioner	l'après-shampooing	*lah-preh-shahm-po-ing*
lotion / moisturizer	lotion	*loh-syon*
mirror	miroir	*mee-rwahr*

The water is ...
L'eau est ...
loh eh ...

freezing.	glacée.	*glah-say.*
too hot.	trop chaude.	*troh shode.*
just right.	parfaite.	*par-fet.*
brown.	marron.	*mah-rohn.*

I need to ...
J'ai besoin ...
zhay be-zwahn ...

brush my teeth.
de me laver les dents.
duh muh lah-vay lay dahn.

floss.
d'utiliser du fil dentaire.
dew-tee-lee-zay dew feel dahn-tair.

do my hair.
de me coiffer.
duh muh kwah-fay.

brush my hair.
de me brosser les cheveux.
duh muh bro-say lay shuh-vuh.

comb my hair.
de me peigner.
duh muh peh-nyay.

dry my hair.
de me sécher les cheveux.
duh muh say-shay lay shuh-vuh.

put on makeup.
de me maquiller.
duh muh mah-kee-yay.

clean out my earwax.
de me nettoyer les oreilles.
duh muh ne-twah-yay lay-zo-rey.

Have you seen...
Est-ce que tu as (vous avez) vu ...
es kuh tew ah (voo-zah-vay) vew ...

my toothbrush?
ma brosse à dents?
mah bros ah dahn?

the hair dryer?
le sèche-cheveux?
luh sesh shuh-vuh?

Getting Ready

I don't have anything to wear.
Je n'ai rien à me mettre.
zhuh nay ryahn ah muh metr.

I'm ready!
Je suis prêt(e)!
zhuh swee preh (prêt)!

I need more time.
J'ai besoin de plus de temps.
zhay be-zwahn duh plew duh tahn.

[Five] more minutes.
J'ai besoin de [cinq] minutes.
zhay be-zwahn duh [sank] mee-newt.

I'll meet you ...
Je vous (te) rejoins ...
zhuh voo (tuh) ruh-zhwahn ...

outside.
à l'extérieur.
ah lex-tay-ryoor.

in the lobby.
à l'accueil.
ah lahk-koy.

at the restaurant.
au restaurant.
au res-toh-rahn.

You look great.
Vous êtes (Tu es) superbe.
voo-zet (tew eh) sew-pairb.

You've aged well.
Vous avez (Tu as) bien vieilli.
voo-zah-vay (tew ah) byahn vyeh-yee.

I look terrible!
Je suis affreux (affreuse)!
zhuh swee-zahf-fruh [-zahf-fruhz]!

Is this outfit appropriate?
Cette tenu est appropriée?
set tuh-new eh ah-pro-pree-yay?

Do you have ...
Est-ce que vous avez (tu as) ...
es kuh voo-zah-vay (tew ah) ...

> **money?**
> de l'argent?
> *duh lahr-zhahn?*

> **your ID?**
> une piece d'identité?
> *ewn pyes dee-dahn-tee-tay?*

~~~~~~

I can't find ...
Je ne trouve pas ...
zhuh nuh troov pah ...

> **my purse.**
> mon sac à main.
> *mon sahk ah man.*

> **my wallet.**
> mon portefeuille.
> *mon por-tuh-foy.*

> **my keys.**
> mes clés.
> *meh klay.*

~~~~~~

Are you bringing [a bag]?
Vous apportez (Tu apportes) [un sac]?
voo-zahp-por-tay (tew ahp-port) [uhn sahk]?

GROOMING AND PRIMPING

5

Making Plans

What are you up to tonight?
Qu'est ce que vous faites (tu fais) ce soir?
kess kuh voo fet (tew feh) suh swahr?

You feel like doing something?
Est-ce que vous voulez (tu veux) faire
quelque chose?
*es kuh voo voo-lay (tew vuh) fair
kel-kuh shoze?*

Yeah, I'd love to.
Oui, je veux bien.
wee, zhuh vuh byahn.

Maybe.
Peut-être.
puh-tetr.

Not sure yet.
Je ne sais pas encore.
zhuh nuh seh pah ahn-kor.

No, I can't, sorry.
Non, je ne peux pas, désolé(e).
nawn, zhuh nuh puh pah pahday-so-lay.

No, I'm tired.
Non, je suis fatigué(e).
nawn, zhuh swee fah-tee-gay.

I'm staying in.
Non, je reste à la maison.
nawn, zhuh rest ah lah meh-zon.

Call me if it seems fun.
Appelle-moi si ça a l'air bien.
ahp-pel mwah see sah ah lair byahn.

What do you feel like doing?
Qu'est-ce que vous avez (tu as) envie de faire?
kess kuh vooz avay (tew ah) zahn-vee duh fair?

Did you eat yet?
Vous avez (Tu as) déjà mangé?
Vooz avay (tew ah) day-zhah mahn-zhay?

Have you talked to [John]?
Vous avez (Tu as) parlé avec [John]?
Vooz avay (tew ah) par-lay ah-vek [john]?

I'm in the mood for ...
J'ai envie de ...
zahy ahn-vee duh ...

We could ...
On pourrait ...
ohn poo-reh ...

> **go to a movie.**
> aller au cinéma.
> *ah-lay oh see-nay-mah.*

> **go to a show.**
> aller au théâtre.
> *ah-lay oh tay-ahtr.*

> **go out to dinner.**
> aller au restaurant.
> *ah-lay oh res-toh-rahn.*

get drinks.
boire un verre.
bwahr uhn vair.

go on a bender.
aller se soûler la gueule.
ah-lay suh soo-lay lah guhl.

hang out in my room.
rester dans ma chambre.
res-tay dahn mah shahmbr.

Where should we go?
On devrait aller où?
ohn duh-vreh ah-lay oo?

I love that place.
J'adore cet endroit.
zhah-dor set ahn-drwah.

I hate that place.
Je déteste cet endroit.
zhuh day-test set ahn-drwah.

I've never been there.
Je n'y suis jamais allé(e).
zuh nee swee zhah-meh ah-lay.

I heard it gets a good crowd.
J'ai entendu que l'ambiance est sympa.
zhay ahn-tahn-dew kuh lahm-byahns eh sahm-pah.

Is it close by?
C'est près d'ici?
seh preh dee-see?

Is it far?
C'est loin?
seh lwahn?

GOING OUT

What time does it open?
Ça ouvre à quelle heure?
sah oovr ah kel uhr?

What time does it close?
Ça ferme à quelle heure?
sah fairm ah kel uhr?

What time do you want to meet?
On se donne rendez-vous à quelle heure?
ohn suh dun rahn-day-voo ah kel uhr?

How long do you need to get ready?
Vous avez (Tu as) besoin de combien de temps
pour vous (te) préparer?
*Vooz avay (tah) be-zwahn duh kom-byahn duh tahn poor
voo (tuh) pray-pah-ray?*

I'm free at ...
Je suis libre à ...
zhuh swee leebr ah ...

Okay, I'll call you at ...
D'accord, je vous appelle (t'appelle) à ...
dak-kor, zhuh voo zah-pel (tah-pel) ah ...

What are you going to wear?
Qu'est-ce que vous allez (tu vas) mettre?
kess kuh voo zah-lay (tew vah) metr?

What should I wear?
Je devrais m'habiller comment?
zhuh duh-vray ma-bee-yay ko-mahn?

Do I have to dress formally?
Est-ce que je dois m'habiller bien?
es kuh zhuh dwah mah-bee-yay byahn?

Do we need a reservation?
Est-ce que nous avons besoin de réserver?
es kuh noozah-von be-zwahn duh ray-zair-vay?

Is there dancing?
Est-ce qu'on peut danser?
es kon puh dahn-say?

Do they ask for ID?
Est-ce qu'ils demandent une pièce d'identité?
es keel duh-mahnd ewn pyes dee-dahn-tee-tay?

What time does the [show] start?
[Le spectacle] commence à quelle heure?
[luh spek-takl] ko-mahns ah kel uhr?

How late will you be out?
Vous sortez (Tu sors) tard?
voo sor-tay (tew sor) tar?

I have something to do in the morning.
J'ai quelque chose à faire demain matin.
zhay kel-kuh shoze ah fair duh-man mah-tan.

Let's make it an early night.
On ne va pas rester tard.
ohn vah pah res-tay tar.

Let's go wild!
Lâchons-nous!
lah-shon noo!

Where do you want to meet?
On se donne rendez-vous où?
onz-dun rahn-day vooz oo?

Let's meet at ...
On se voit à ...
on s-vwah ah ...

What street is it on?
C'est dans quelle rue?
seh dahn kel rew?

I'll meet you there.
Je vous (te) rejoins là-bas
zhuh voo (tuh) ruh-zhwahn lah-bah.

Call me if you get lost.
Appelle-moi si vous vous perdez (tu te perds).
ah-pel mwah see voo voo pair-day (tew tuh pair).

Where are you?
Vous êtes (Tu es) où?
voo zet (tew eh) oo?

I'm running late.
Je suis en retard.
zhuh swee zahn ruh-tar.

I'll be there in [ten] minutes.
Je serai là dans [dix] minutes.
zhuh suh-ray lah dahn [dee] mee-newt.

At the Bar

I love this place!
J'aime bien cet endroit!
zhem byahn seh tahn-drwah!

Let's stay a little longer.
Restons encore un peu.
res-ton zahn-kor uhn puh.

Do you see a table anywhere?
Est-ce que vous voyez (tu vois) une table quelque part?
es kuh voo vwah-yay (tew vwah) ewn tahbl kel-kuh par?

I'll be by the bar.
Je serai au bar.
zhuh suh-ray oh bar.

This place sucks.
Cet endroit est nul.
seh tahn-drwah eh newl.

Let's go somewhere else.
Allons ailleurs.
ah-lon   zah-yuhr.

Let's go back to that other place.
Retournons à l'autre endroit.
ruh-toor-non zah lohtr ahn-drwah.

Let's go home.
Rentrons.
rahn-tron.

I'm tired.
Je suis fatigué(e).
zhuh swee fah-tee-gay.

I'm not tired yet.
Je ne suis pas encore fatigué(e).
zhuh nuh swee pah zahn-kor fah-tee-gay.

I'm just getting started.
Je commence à peine à m'amuser.
zhuh ko-mahns ah pen ah mah-mew-zay.

I'm out of cash.
Je n'ai plus d'argent.
zhuh nay plew dar-zhahn.

This place is too expensive.
C'est trop cher ici.
seh troh shair ee-see.

Can you loan me some money?
Est-ce que vous pourriez (tu pourrais) me prêter de l'argent?
es kuh voo poor-yay (tew poo-reh) muh preh-tay duh lar-zhahn?

Is there an ATM around here?
Est-ce qu'il y a un distributeur dans le coin?
es keel yah uhn dees-tree-bew-tur dahn luh kwahn?

Do you have a light?
Vous avez (Tu as) du feu?
voo-zah-vay (tew ah) dew fuh?

Do you have a cigarette?
Est-ce que vous avez (tu as) une cigarette?
es kuh voo-zah-vay (tew ah) ewn see-gah-ret?

Do you want a drink?
Vous voulez (Tu veux) un verre?
voo voo-lay (tew vuh) uhn vair?

What do you like to drink?
Qu'est-ce que vous voulez (tu veux) boire?
kess kuh voo voo-lay (tew vuh) bwahr?

7 Pairing Up

Pickup Lines

Come here often?
Vous venez (Tu viens) souvent ici?
voo ven-ay (tew vyahn) soo-vahn ee-see?

**Is everyone from [France] as pretty /
handsome as you?**
Tout le monde en [France] est aussi belle /
beau que toi?
*tool mohnd ahn [Frahns] eh oh-see bel /
boh kuh twah?*

**Are you sure you're not from heaven?
Because you look like an angel.**
Vous êtes (T'es) sure / sûr que vous ne venez
(tu ne viens) pas du ciel? Parce que vous rassem-
blez (tu rassembles) à une ange.
*vooz et (teh) sewr kuh voo nuh veh-nay
(tew nuh vyahn) pahdew syel? pars kuh voo re-sahm-
blay (tew re-sahmbl) ah ewn ahnzh.*

Don't fall in love with me. I'm bad news.
Tombez (Tombe) pas amoureuse (amoureux) de
moi. Je suis dangereux (dangereuse).
*tow-mbay (towmb) pah ah-moo-ruhz (ah-moo-ruh) duh
mwah. zhuh swee dahn-zhuh-ruh (dahn-zhuh-ruhz).*

Let's get to know each other.
Faisons connaissance.
feh-zon ko-neh-sahns.

Tell me about yourself.
Racontez-moi (Raconte-moi) votre (ta) vie.
rah-kon-tay-mwha (rah-kont-mwha) vohtr (tah) vee.

What do you do?
Vous faites (Tu fais) quoi?
voo feht (tew feh) kwah?

What music/films/books do you like?
Vous aimez (Tu aimes) quelle musique /
quels films / quels livres?
*vooz emay (tew em) kel mew-zeek /
kel feelm / kel leevr?*

Are you from here?
Vous venez (Tu viens) d'ici?
voo ven-ay (tew vyahn) dee-see?

Where do you live?
Vous habitez (Tu habites) où?
vooz ah-beet-ayz (tew ah-beet) oo?

Cool!	Cool!	*kool!*
Great!	Génial!	*zhay-nyahl!*
Fascinating!	C'est fascinant!	*seh fah-see-nahn!*
Me too!	Moi aussi!	*mwah oh-see!*

You're ...
Vous êtes (Tu es) ...
voo zets (tew eh) ...

pretty.	jolie.	*zho-lee.*
beautiful.	belle.	*bel.*
handsome.	beau.	*boh.*
stunning.	magnifique.	*mah-nyee-feek.*

You are the most beautiful woman/man I've ever seen.
Vous êtes (Tu es) la plus belle femme / le plus beau homme que j'ai jamais vue.
vooz ets (tew eh) lah plew bel fahm / luh plew boh um kuh zhay zhah-meh vew.

I like you.
Je vous aime (t'aime) bien.
zhuh voo (zem (tem) byahn.

You seem nice.
Vous avez (Tu as) l'air sympa.
vooz avay (tew ah) lair sem-pah.

You have such ...
Vous avez (Tu as) de si ...
Vooz avay (tew ah) duh see ...

beautiful eyes.
beaux yeux.
boh-zyuh.

beautiful hair.
beaux cheveux.
boh shuh-vuh.

beautiful hands.
belles mains.
bel man.

I'm interested in you.
Vous (Tu) m'intéresse.
voo (tew) man-tay-res.

Do you have a [boyfriend / girlfriend]?
Vous avez (Tu as) un [copain] / une [copine]?
Vooz avay (tew ah) zuhn [ko-pan] / ewn [ko-peen]?

My [boyfriend/girlfriend] is out of town (this weekend).
Mon [copain] / Ma [copine] n'est pas là (ce week-end).
mon [ko-pan] / mah [ko-peen] neh pah lah (suh week-END).

Rejection

I'm here with my [boyfriend / girlfriend].
Je suis là avec mon [copain] / ma [copine].
zhuh swee lah ah-vek mon [ko-pan] / mah [ko-peen].

I'm sorry, but I'm not interested.
Désolée, mais ce ne m'intéresse pas.
day-zo-lay, meh suh nuh man-tay-res pah.

You're just not my type.
Vous n'êtes (Tu n'es) pas mon genre.
voo net (tew neh) pah mon zhahn-r.

Please leave me alone.
Laissez-moi (Laisse-moi) tranquille, s'il vous (te) plaît.
leh-say-mwah (less-mwah) trahn-keel, see voo (tuh) pleh.

Get away from me!
Casse-toi!
kahs twah!

Security!
Sécurité!
say-kew-ree-tay!

Are you gay?
Vous êtes (Tu es) gay?
vooz et (tew eh) gay?

I'm gay.
Je suis gay.
zhuh swee gay.

PAIRING UP

7

I'm straight.
Je suis hétéro.
zhuh swee ay-tay-roh.

It's a pity you aren't gay.
C'est dommage que vous ne soyez (tu ne sois) pas gay.
seh do-mahzh kuh voo nuh soy-ay (tew nuh swah) pah gay.

I'm bisexual.
Je suis bi.
zhu swee bee.

I'm transgendered.
Je suis transsexuel.
zhuh swee trahn-sek-sew-el.

I used to be a [man / woman]!
Avant, j'étais un [homme] / une [femme]!
ah-vahn, zhay-teh uhn [um] / ewn [fahm]!

Love at First Sight

Can I stay over?
Je peux rester cette nuit?
zhuh puh res-tay set nwee?

I want you to stay over.
Je veux que vous restiez (tu restes).
zhuh vuh kuh voo rest-yay (tew rest).

Let's spend the night together.
Passons la nuit ensemble.
pah-sohn lah nwee ahn-sahmbl.

We can watch the sun rise.
On peut regarder le lever du soleil.
on puh ruh-gar-day luh luh-vay dew so-ley.

Kiss me.
Embrassez-moi (Embrasse-moi).
ahm-brahsay-mwah (ahm-brahs-mwah).

It's better if you go home.
C'est mieux que vous rentriez (tu rentres).
seh myuh kuh voo rahn-tree-yay (tew rahntr).

I'd better go.
Je devrais partir.
zhuh duh-vray par-teer.

I think we should stop.
Je pense qu'on devrait arrêter.
zhuh pahns kon duh-vray ah-reh-tay.

I have to go home now.
Je dois rentrer maintenant.
zhuh dwah rahn-tray mat-nahn.

I had a great time.
J'ai passé un bon moment.
zhay pah-say uhn bon moh-mahn.

Thanks for a lovely evening.
Merci pour cette soirée sympa.
mair-see poor set swah-ray sam-pah.

Here's my number.
Voilà mon numéro.
vwah-lah mon new-may-roh.

I'm here for [three] more days.
Je reste encore [trois] jours.
zhuh rest ahn-kor [trwah] zhoor.

Can we meet tomorrow?
On peut se voir demain?
on puh suh vwahr duh-man?

Can I see you again?
Je peux vous (te) revoir?
zhuh puh voo (tuh) ruh-vwahr?

What is your email address?

Quelle est votre adresse mél?

Kel ay vote rah-dress mell / ay-mell?

When can I see you?

Quand est-ce que je pourrais vous (te) voir?

kahn es kuh zhuh poo-reh voo (tuh) vwahr?

Where do you want to meet?

Vous voulez (Tu veux) qu'on se voit où?

voo voo-lay (tew vuh) kon suh vwah oo?

~~~~~~

Are you seeing someone else?

Vous êtes (Tu es) avec quelqu'un?

voo zeht (tew eh) ah-vek kel-kuhn?

He / She's just a friend.

C'est juste un ami. / une amie.

seh jewst uhn ah-mee. / ewn ah-mee.

I think we should just be friends.

Je pense qu'on devrait rester amis.

zhuh pahns kon duh-vreh res-tay ah-mee.

~~~~~~

I love you!

Je t'aime!

zhuh tem!

I'm in love with you!

Je suis amoureux (amoureuse) de vous (toi)!

zhuh swee ah-moo-ruh (ah-moo-ruhz) duh voo (twah)!

You should come visit me.

Vous devriez (Tu devrais) venir me voir.

voo dev-ree-yay (tew duh-vray) vuh-neer muh vwahr.

Let's be pen pals.

Soyons correspondants.

swah-yon ko-res-pon-dahn.

I promise to write you.

Je (vous écris) t'écris, je vous (te) le promet.

zhu vooz ay-kree (tay-kree), zhu voo (tuh) luh pro-meh.

I'll never forget you.

Je ne vous oublierai (t'oublierai) jamais.

zhuh nuh vooz oo-blee-eh-ray (too-blee-eh-ray) zhah-meh.

Our time together has meant a lot to me.

Le moment qu'on a passé signifie
beaucoup pour moi.

*luh mo-mahn kon ah pah-say see-nyee-fee
boh-koo poor mwah.*

What was your name again?

Vous vous appelez (Tu t'appelles) comment
déjà?

voo voo zah-pel-ay (tew tah-pel) ko-mahn day-zhah?

Seeing the Sights

Sights

I'd like to see ...
J'aimerais voir ...
zhem-reh vwahr ...

> **the museum.**
> le musée.
> *luh mew-zay.*
>
> **the art gallery.**
> la galerie d'art.
> *lah gahl-ree dar.*
>
> **the palace.**
> le palais.
> *luh pah-leh.*
>
> **the castle.**
> le château.
> *luh shah-toh.*
>
> **the church.**
> l'église.
> *lay-gleez.*
>
> **the cathedral.**
> la cathédrale.
> *lah kah-tay-drahl.*

the park.
le parc.
luh park.

the gardens.
les jardins.
lay zhar-dan.

the zoo.
le zoo.
luh zoh.

the ruins.
les ruines.
lay rween.

the cemetery.
la cimetière.
lah see-muh-tyear.

some art.
de l'art.
duh lar.

some historical sites.
des sites historiques.
day seet ees-to-reek.

the downtown area.
le centre-ville.
luh sahn-tr-veel.

the historic district.
le quartier historique.
luh kar-tyay ees-to-reek.

the shopping district.
le quartier commerçant.
luh kar-tyay ko-mair-sahn.

the red-light district.
le quartier chaud.
luh kar-tyay shoh.

Do you have any ...

Est-ce que vous avez (tu as) ...
es kuh voo-zah-vay (tew ah) ...

> **brochures?**   des brochures?   *day bro-shure?*
>
> **maps?**   des plans?   *day plahn?*
>
> **suggestions?**   des suggestions?   *day sew-zhes-tyon?*

I'd like to go on a ...

J'aimerais faire une ...
zhem-reh fair ewn ...

> **walking tour.**
> visite guidée à pied.
> *vee-zeet ghee-day ah pyeh.*
>
> **guided tour.**
> visite guidée.
> *vee-zeet ghee-day.*
>
> **bus tour.**
> visite guidée en bus.
> *vee-zeet ghee-day ahn bewss.*
>
> **boat tour.**
> visite guidée en bateau.
> *vee-zeet ghee-day ahn bah-toh.*

Where can I hire a guide / translator?

Où est-ce que je peux trouver un guide /
un traducteur?
oo es kuh zhuh puh troo-vay uhn gheed / trah-dook-tur?

What's the nicest part of the city?

Où est la partie de la ville la plus sympa?
oo eh lah par-tee duh lah veel lah plew sam-pah?

What's your favorite neighborhood?

Quel est votre (ton) quartier préféré?

kel eh votr (tawn) kar-tyay pray-fay-ray?

Is this area safe?

Ce quartier est sûr?

suh kar-tyay eh sewr?

What should I see if I'm here only one day?

Qu'est-ce que je devrais voir si j'étais là pour un seul jour?

kess kuh zhuh duh-vray vwahr see zhay-teh lah poor uhn suhl zhoor?

Where's the best place to watch the sunset / sunrise?

Où est le meilleur endroit pour regarder le lever / le coucher du soleil?

oo eh luh mey-yuhr ahn-drwah poor ruh-gar-day luh luh-vay / luh koo-shay dew so-ley?

Calling Ahead

Where does the tour start?

Où commence la visite?

oo ko-mahns lah vee-zeet?

What time does it start?

Ça commence à quelle heure?

sah ko-mahns ah kel uhr?

How long is it?

Ça dûre combien de temps?

sah dure kom-byahn duh tahn?

What stops does it make?

Quels sont les arrêts?

kel son lay-zah-reh?

Do I have to reserve a spot?
Est-ce que je dois réserver une place?
es kuh zhuh dwah ray-zair-vay ewn plahs?

What hours are you open?
Quels sont vos horaires d'ouverture?
kel son voh-zo-rair doo-vair-ture?

When do you close?
Vous fermez à quelle heure?
voo fair-may ah kel uhr?

What do you charge for admission?
Quel est le prix d'entrée?
kel eh luh pree dahn-tray?

Is there a student discount?
Est-ce qu'il y a une remise pour les étudiants?
es keel yah ewn ruh-meez poor lay-zay-tew-dyahn?

Is there a group discount?
Est-ce que il y a une réduction pour les groupes?
es keel yah ewn ray-duke-syon poor lay groop?

Cultural Stuff

Let's go to ...
Allons ...
ah-lon ...

the theater.
au théatre.
oh tay-ahtr.

the movies.
au cinéma.
oh see-nay-mah.

a show.
au spectacle.
oh spek-takl.

a concert.
au concert.
oh   kon-sair.

the opera.
à l'opéra.
ah   loh-pay-rah.

an exhibit.
à une exposition.
ah   ewn   ex-po-zee-syon.

a soccer game.
à un match de foot.
ah   uhn   mahch   duh   foot.

a bullfight.
à une corrida.
ah   ewn   ko-ree-dah.

Where's the movie playing?
Le film se joue où?
luh   feelm   suh   zhoo   oo?

What time does the show start?
Le spectacle commence à quelle heure?
luh   spek-takl   ko-mahns   ah   kel uhr?

How much are the tickets?
Les billets coûtent combien?
lay   bee-yeh   koot   kom-byahn?

Do you have any tickets left for tonight?
Est-ce qu'il reste des places pour ce soir?
es   keel   rest   day   plahs   poor   suh   swahr?

Is tonight's performance sold out?
C'est complet pour ce soir?
seh   kom-pleh   poor   suh   swahr?

Money

I want to go shopping.
Je voudrais faire les magasins.
zhuh voo-dreh fair lay mah-gah-zan.

Where can I change money?
Où est-ce que je peux changer de l'argent?
oo es kuh zhuh puh shahn-zhay duh lar-zhahn?

What's the exchange rate?
Quel est le taux de change?
kel eh luh toh duh shahzh?

Is there a(n) ... around here?
Est-ce qu'il y a ... dans le coin?
es keel yah ... dahn luh kwahn?

> **bank**
> une banque
> *ewn bahnk*

> **ATM**
> un distributeur
> *uhn dees-tree-bew-tur*

> **store**
> un magasin
> *uhn mah-gah-zan*

market
un marché
uhn mar-shay

mall
un centre commerciale
uhn sahntr ko-mair-syahl

department store
un grand magasin
uhn grahn mah-gah-zan

grocery store
une épicerie
ewn ay-pee-sree

supermarket
un supermarché
uhn sew-pair-mar-shay

drugstore / pharmacy
une pharmacie
ewn far-mah-see

bookstore
une librarie
ewn lee-bray-ree

souvenir shop
un magasin de souvenirs
uhn mah-gah-zan duh soo-vuh-neer

casino
un casino
uhn ka-zee-no

At the Store

I need to buy ...
J'ai besoin d'acheter ...
zhay be-zwahn dahsh-tay ...

Do you sell ... ?
Est-ce que vous vendez ... ?
es kuh voo vahn-day ...?

I'm looking for ...
Je cherche ...
zhuh shairsh ...

clothes.	des vêtements.	*day vet-mahn.*
souvenirs.	des souvenirs.	*day soo-vuh-neer.*
postcards.	des cartes postales.	*day kart pos-tahl.*
stamps.	des timbres.	*day tembr.*
a map.	un plan.	*uhn plahn.*
a guidebook.	un guide.	*uhn gheed.*
an umbrella.	un parapluie.	*uhn pah-rah-plwee.*

I need a gift for ...
J'ai besoin d'un cadeau pour ...
zhay be-zwahn duhn kah-doh poor ...

my friend
un ami./ une amie.
uhn / ewn ah-mee.

my parents.
mes parents.
meh pah-rahn.

my brother. / sister.
mon frère. / ma soeur.
mon frair. / mah suhr.

my boyfriend. / girlfriend.
mon copain. / ma copine.
mon ko-pen. / mah ko-peen.

Can you suggest anything?
Vous pouvez me conseiller quelque chose?
voo poo-vay muh kon-se-yey kel-kuh shoze?

I'm just browsing, thanks.
Je regarde juste, merci.
zhuh ruh-gard zhewst, mair-see.

That's ...
C'est ...
seh ...

nice.	bien / mignon.	*byahn / mee-nyon.*
perfect.	parfait.	*par-feh.*
beautiful.	beau.	*boh.*
lovely.	joli.	*jo-lee.*
ugly.	moche.	*mosh.*
hideous.	horrible. / affreux.	*aw-reebl / ah-fruh.*
divine.	divin. / fabuleux.	*dee-van / fah-bew-luh.*

GOING BROKE

9

I like it.
Je l'aime bien.
zhuh lem byahn.

I don't like it.
Je ne l'aime pas.
zhuh nuh lem pah.

Is it handmade?
C'est fait à la main?
seh fe ah lah man?

Can I try it on?
Je peux l'essayer?
zhuh puh le-seh-yay?

How does this look?
Ça me va?
sah muh vah?

It doesn't look good on me.
Ça ne me va pas.
sah nuh muh vah pah.

It doesn't fit me.
Ce n'est pas la bonne taille.
suh neh pah lah bun tai.

Do you have something ...
Est-ce que vous avez quelque chose ...
es kuh voo-zah-vay kel-kuh shoze ...

> **cheaper?**
> de moins cher?
> *duh mwahn shair?*

> **fancier?**
> de plus habillé?
> *duh plew-zah-bee-yay?*

in a bigger size?
dans une plus grande taille?
dahn-zewn plew grahn-d tahy?
in a smaller size?
dans une plus petite taille?
dahn-zewn plew puh-teet tahy?

in a different color?
dans une autre couleur?
dahn-zewn ohtr koo-lur?

Is anything on sale?
Est-ce qu'il y a des soldes?
es keel yah day sold?

Haggling

How much does this cost?
Ça coûte combien?
sah koot kom-byahn?

That's ...
C'est ...
seh ...

a bargain.
bon marché.
bon mar-shay.

too expensive.
trop cher.
troh shair.

a complete ripoff.
du vol.
dew vol.

Can I get a lower price?
Est-ce que je pourrais l'avoir pour moins cher?
es kuh zhuh poo-reh lah-vwahr poor mwahn share?

I'll offer you half that.
Je vous en propose la moité.
zhuh vooz ahn pro-poz lah mwah-tay.

Paying

I have cash.
J'ai des espèces.
zhay day-zes-pes.

I don't have change.
Je n'ai pas de monnaie.
zhuh nay pah duh mon-nay.

Do you take ...
Est-ce que vous prenez ...
es kuh voo pruh-nay ...

credit cards?
des cartes de credit?
day kart duh cre-dee?

checks?
les chèques?
lay shek?

traveler's checks?
les travelers chèques?
lay trah-vlairs shek?

Can you wrap it for me?

Est-ce que vous pourriez faire un paquet
cadeau?

es kuh voo poo-ryay fair uhn pah-keh kah-doh?

Can I get it shipped home?

Pourriez-vous le faire envoyer aux Etats-Unis?

poor-yay voo luh fair ahn-vwah-yay oh-zay-tahs-yoo-nee?

Can I get it delivered?

Ça pourrait être livré?

sah poo-reh etr lee-vray?

The address is _____.

L'addresse est _____.

lah-dress eh _____.

I need to return this.

Je voudrais échanger ceci, s'il vous plaît.

zhuh voo-dreh ay-shahn-zhay suh-see, see voo pleh.

Doing Nothing

What do you feel like doing?
Qu'est ce que vous avez (tu as) envie de faire?
kes kuh vooz avay (tew ah) ahn-vee duh fair?

Do you play ...
Est-ce que vous jouez (tu joues) ...
es kuh voo zhoo-ay (tew zhoo) ...

cards?	aux cartes?	*oh kart?*
checkers?	aux dames?	*oh dahm?*
chess?	aux échecs?	*oh-zay-shek?*

I win.
J'ai gagné.
zhay ga-nyay.

You lose.
Vous avez (Tu as) perdu.
vooz avay (tew ah) pair-dew.

Let's play again.
On rejoue.
on ruh-zhoo.

This is fun.
C'est amusant / marrant.
seh tah-mew-zahn / mah-rahn.

You're learning fast.
Vous apprenez (Tu apprends) vite.
voo zah-pren-ay (tew ah-prahn) veet.

You suck at this.
Vous êtes (Tu es) nul à ce jeu.
voo zet (tew eh) newl ah suh zhuh.

~~~~~~~~~~~~~~~~~~~~~~~~~~~~~~~~~~

I just want to ...
Je voudrais simplement ...
zhuh voo-dreh sam-pluh-mahn ...

stay in.
rester à la maison.
res-tay ah lah meh-zon.

relax.
me reposer.
muh ruh-po-zay.

sit at a café.
me poser dans un café.
muh po-zay dahn-zuhn kah-fay.

go read somewhere.
aller quelque part pour lire.
ah-lay kel-kuh par poor leer.

go for a walk.
aller me balader.
ah-lay muh bah-lah-day.

The Beach

Let's go to the beach.
Allons à la plage.
ah-lon zah lah plahzh.

Where can I buy ...
Où est-ce que je peux acheter ...
oo es kuh zhuh puh ah-shuh-tay ...

> **a beach towel?**
> une serviette de bain?
> *ewn sair-vyet duh ban?*

> **a beach chair?**
> un transat?
> *uhn trahn-zaht?*

> **a beach umbrella?**
> un parasol?
> *uhn pah-rah-sol?*

> **a swimsuit?**
> un maillot de bain?
> *uhn my-yo duh ban?*

> **flip-flops?**
> des thongs?
> *day tong?*

> **sunscreen?**
> de la crème solaire?
> *duh lah krem so-lair?*

> **a trashy novel?**
> un roman de gare?
> *uhn ro-mahn duh gar?*

I need to put on sunscreen.
J'ai besoin de mettre de la crème solaire.
zhay be-zwahn duh metr duh lah krem so-lair.

Am I getting burned?
Est-ce que je suis en train de brûler?
es kuh zhuh swee-zahn tran duh brew-lay?

You're getting burned.
Vous êtes (Tu es) en train de brûler.
voo zet (tew eh) ahn tran duh brew-lay.

You're ...
Vous êtes ... / Tu es ...
voo-zet ... / tew eh ...

> **tan.**
> bronzé(e).
> *bron-zay.*

> **sunburned.**
> brulé(e). / rouge.
> *brew-lay. / roozh.*

> **really white.**
> très pale.
> *treh pahl.*

Can you swim here?
On peut nager ici?
on puh nah-zhay ee-see?

Is there a lifeguard?
Il y a un surveillant de baignade?
eel yah uhn sur-ve-yahn duh beh-nyahd?

How deep is the water?
L'eau est-elle très profonde?
loh eh-tel treh pro-fond?

Let's go swimming.
Allons se baigner.
ah-lon suh beh-nyay.

Come on in.
Venez. (Viens.)
ven-ay. (vyahn.)

~~~~~~~~~~~~~~~~~~~~~~~~~~~~~~~~

The water's ...
L'eau est ...
loh eh ...

> **great.**
> bonne.
> *bun.*
>
> **warm.**
> chaude.
> *shode.*
>
> **cold.**
> froide.
> *frwahd.*
>
> **shallow.**
> (n'est pas) profonde.
> *(neh pah) pro-fond.*
>
> **deep.**
> profonde.
> *pro-fond.*
>
> **rough.**
> agitée.
> *ah-zhee-tay.*

> **full of jellyfish.**
> pleine de méduses.
> *plen duh may-dewz.*
>
> **teeming with sharks.**
> infestée de requins.
> *an-fes-tay duh ruh-kan.*

Don't swim out too far.
N'allez (Ne va) pas trop loin.
nah-lay (nuh vah) pas troh lwahn.

Where's the nude beach?
Où se trouve la plage nudiste?
oo suh troov lah plahzh new-deest?

~~~~~~~~~~~~~~~~~~~~~~~~~~~~~~~~~~~~~

Let's go ...
Allons ...
ah-lon ...

snorkeling.
faire du snorkeling.
fair duh snor-ke-leeng.

scuba diving.
faire du plonger sous marine.
fair dew plon-zhay soo mah-reen.

fishing.
pêcher.
puh-shay.

rent a boat.
louer un bateau.
loo-ay uhn bah-toh.

rent a Jet Ski.
louer un Jet Ski.
loo-ay uhn zhet skee.

~~~~~~~~~~~~~~~~~~~~~~~~~~~~~~~~~~~~~

Where is the ...
Où est ...
oo eh ...

dock?
le ponton?
luh pon-ton?

dive shop?
le magasin de plonger?
luh mah-gah-zan duh plon-zhay?

marina?
le centre nautique?
luh sahntr noh-teek?

~~~~~~

Can I rent ... here?
Je peux louer ... ici?
zhuh puh loo-ay ... ee-see?

> **equipment**
> des équipements
> *day-zay-keep-mahn*

> **a wetsuit**
> une combinaison
> *ewn kom-bee-neh-zon*

> **a mask**
> un masque de plonger
> *uhn mahsk duh plon-zhay*

Sports

Do you like to ...
Vous aimez (Tu aimes)...
voo-ze-may (tew em) ...

> **play sports?**
> faire du sport?
> *fair dew spor?*

> **play soccer?**
> jouer au foot?
> *zhoo-ay oh foot?*

> **play tennis?**
> jouer au tennis?
> *zhoo-ay oh te-neess?*

play basketball?
jouer au basket?
zhoo-ay oh bahs-ket?

play golf?
jouer au golf?
zhoo-ay oh gulf?

swim?
nager?
nah-zhay?

bike?
faire du vélo?
fair dew vay-loh?

jog?
faire du jogging?
fair dew zho-geeng?

ski?
faire du ski?
fair dew skee?

do yoga?
faire du yoga?
fair dew yo-gah?

go sailing?
faire du bateau à voile?
fair dew bah-toh ah vwahl?

go skating?
patiner?
pah-tee-nay?

go diving?
plonger?
plon-zhay?

go horseback riding?
faire de l'équitation? / du cheval?
fair duh lay-kee-tah-syon? / dew shuh-vahl?

I'm not very good at this.
Je ne suis pas très doué(e) pour cela.
zhuh nuh swee pah treh doo-ay poor suh-lah.

You're great at this!
Vous le faites (Tu le fait) bien!
Voo luh fet (tew luh feh) byahn!

Let's race to the end.
Faisons la course jusqu'au bout.
feh-zon lah koors zhews-koh boo.

This is fun.
C'est chouette.
seh shwet.

I'm tired.
Je suis fatigué(e).
zhuh swee fah-tee-gay.

I'd like to go to the gym.
J'aimerais aller à la salle de sport.
zhem-rah ah-lay ah lah sahl duh spor.

Is there a gym around here?
Il y a une salle de sport près d'ici?
eel yah ewn sahl duh spor preh dee-see?

Do you have ...
Est-ce que vous avez ...
es kuh voo-zah-vay ...

> ### free weights?
> des altères?
> *day-zahl-tair?*

> ### cardio equipment?
> des machines de cardio-training?
> *day mah-sheen duh kar-dee-o tre-neeng?*

a pool?
une piscine?
ewn pee-seen?

a sauna?
un sauna?
uhn soh-nah?

a treadmill?
des trépigneuses?
day tray-pee-nyuhz?

aerobics?
des séances d'aérobique?
day say-ahns dair-o-beek?

personal trainers?
des entraîneurs? / moniteurs particuliers?
day-zahn-tre-nur? / day mo-nee-tur par-tee-kew-lyay?

classes?
des classes?
day klahs?

How much is a ...
Combien coûte ...
kom-byahn koot ...

pass?
un laisser-passer?
uhn le-say pah-say?

day?
une journée?
ewn zhoor-nay?

week?
une semaine?
ewn suh-men?

month?
un mois?
uhn mwah?

year?
un an?
uhn ahn?

Renting a Car

Where can I rent a car?
Est-ce que je peux louer une voiture?
oo es kuh juh puh loo-ay ewn vwah-ture?

What's the daily rate?
Combien ça coûte par jour?
kom-byahn sah koot par zhoor?

How much is insurance?
L'assurance coûte combien?
lah-sew-rahns koot kom-byahn?

Here's my license.
Voilà mon permit.
vwah-lah mon pair-mee.

There's a dent in it.
Il y a un choc dessus.
eel yah uhn shok duh-sew.

The paint is scratched.
La peinture est éraflée.
lah pan-ture eh tay-rah-flay.

Where can I buy gas?
Où est-ce que je peux acheter de l'essence?
oo es kuh zhuh puh ash-tay duh les-sahns?

stop	stop	*stop*
yield	cédez le passage	*say-day luh pahs-sazh*
one-way	sens unique	*sahns ew-neek*
detour	déviation	*day-vee-ah-syon*
toll	péages	*pay-ahzh*
parking	parking	*par-keeng*

The Outdoors

Do you know good places for ...
Vous connaissez (Tu connais) des endroits pour ...
voo ko-nes-say (tew ko-nay) day-zahn-drwah poor ...

hiking?
faire des randonnées?
fair day rahn-do-nay?

mountain biking?
faire du VTT?
fair dew vay-tay-tay?

rock climbing?
faire de l'escalade?
fair duh les-kah-lahd?

seeing animals?
voir des animaux?
vwahr day-zah-nee-moh?

I need to rent ...
J'ai besoin de louer ...
zhay be-zwahn duh loo-ay ...

a tent.
une tente.
ewn tahnt.

a sleeping bag.
un sac de couchage.
uhn sahk duh koo-shahzh.

hiking boots.
des chaussures de randonée.
day shoh-sewr duh ranh-do-nay.

a flashlight.
une lampe de poche.
ewn lahmp duh posh.

a backpack.
un sac à dos.
uhn sahk ah doh.

a mountain bike.
un VTT.
uhn vay-tay-tay.

a canteen.
une cantine.
ewn kahn-teen.

Do you have trail maps?
Est-ce que vous avez (tu as) des plans des chemins de randonée?
es kuh voo-zah-vay (tew ah) day plahn day shuh-man duh rahn-do-nay?

Is this trail ...
Cette piste est ...
set peest eh ...

hard?	difficile?	*dee-fee-seel?*
easy?	facile?	*fah-seel?*
hilly?	montagneuse?	*mon-tah-nyuhz?*
flat?	plate?	*plaht?*
well-marked?	bien indiquée?	*byahn an-dee-kay?*
scenic?	pittoresque?	*peet-to-resk?*
long?	longue?	*longg?*
short?	courte?	*koort?*
grueling?	épuisante?	*ay-pwee-zahnt?*

Is the water safe to drink?
L'eau est-elle potable?
loh eh-tel poh-tahbl?

What's the weather supposed to be like ...
Quel temps est prévu pour ...
kel tahn eh pray-vew poor ...

today?	aujourd'hui?	*oh-zhoor-dwee?*
tomorrow?	demain?	*duh-man?*
this week?	cette semaine?	*set suh-men?*
this weekend?	ce week-end	*suh week-end*

Is it supposed to …
Est-ce qu'il va y avoir …
es keel vah ee ah-vwahr …

rain?
de la pluie?
duh lah plwee?

snow?
de la neige?
duh lah nezh?

storm?
une tempête?
ewn tahm-pet?

Is it supposed to …
Est-ce qu'il va …
es keel vah …

get cold?
faire froid?
fair frwah?

get hot?
faire chaud?
fair shoh?

Is it supposed to get below freezing?
Est-ce que ça va geler?
es kuh sah vah zhuh-lay?

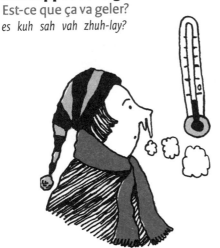

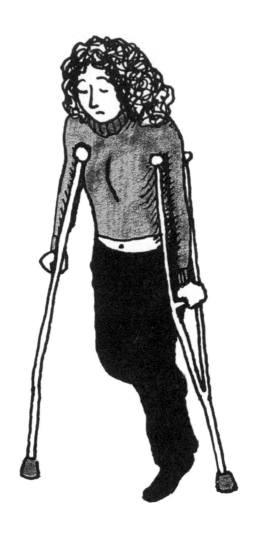

11 Staying Healthy

Ailments

I don't feel well.
Je ne me sens pas bien.
zhuh nuh muh sahn pah byahn.

My ... hurts. / I have a ... ache.
J'ai mal ...
zhay mahl ...

head	à la tête.	*ah lah tet.*
stomach	au ventre.	*oh vahntr.*
throat	à la gorge.	*ah lah gorzh.*
ear	à l'oreille.	*ah lo-rey.*
tooth	à une dent. / aux dents.	*ah ewn dahn. / oh dahn.*
neck	au cou.	*oh koo.*
back	au dos.	*oh doh.*
feet	aux pieds.	*oh pyeh.*

That hurts.
Ça fait mal.
sah feh mahl.

I have pain here.
J'ai mal ici.
zhay mahl ee-see.

I feel ...
Je me sens ...
zhuh muh sahn ...

better.	mieux.	*myuh.*
worse.	pire.	*peer.*
faint.	faible.	*febl.*
weird.	bizarre.	*bee-zar.*

I feel ...
J'ai ...
zhay ...

| **dizzy.** | des vertiges. | *day vair-teezh.* |
| **nauseous.** | la nausée. | *lah noh-zay.* |

I have ...
J'ai ...
zhay ...

a cold.	un rhume.	*uhn rewm.*
a fever.	de la fièvre.	*duh lah fyevr.*
chills.	des frissons.	*day free-son.*
diarrhea.	la diarrée.	*lah dee-ah-ray.*

I threw up.
J'ai vomi.
zhay vo-mee.

I think I broke ...
Je pense que je me suis cassé ...
zhuh pahns kuh zhuh muh swee kah-say ...

> **my arm.**
> le bras.
> *luh brah.*

my finger.
le doigt.
luh dwah.

my wrist.
le poignet.
luh pwah-nyeh.

my toe (my big toe).
le doigt de pied (l'orteil).
luh dwah duh pyeh (lor-tey).

my ankle.
la cheville.
lah shuh-veey.

my foot.
le pied.
luh pyeh.

my leg.
la jambe.
lah zhahmb.

my rib.
une côte.
ewn kote.

my collarbone.
la clavicule.
lah klah-vee-kewl.

Is it broken?
C'est cassé?
seh kah-say?

Is it infected?
C'est infecté?
seh-tan-fek-tay?

Medicine and Prescriptions

I ran out of medicine.
Je n'ai plus de médicaments.
zhuh nay plew duh may-dee-kah-mahn.

I need a refill.
J'ai besoin de remplir à nouveau
mon ordonnance.
*zhay be-zwahn duh rahm-pleer ah noo-voh
mon or-don-nahns.*

I need a new prescription.
J'ai besoin d'une nouvelle ordonnance.
zhay be-zwahn dewn noo-vel or-don-nahns.

I'm allergic ...
Je suis allergique ...
zhuh swee-zahl-lair-zheek ...

> **to ibuprofen.**
> à l'ibuprophen.
> *ah lee-bew-pro-fen.*
>
> **to penicillin.**
> à la pénicilline.
> *ah lah pay-nee-see-leen.*
>
> **to aspirin.**
> à l'aspirine.
> *ah lahs-pee-reen.*
>
> **to bee stings.**
> aux piqûres d'abeille.
> *oh pee-kure dah-bey.*
>
> **to nuts.**
> aux noix.
> *oh nwah.*

I'm diabetic.
Je suis diabétique.
zhuh swee dee-ah-bay-teek.

I have asthma.
J'ai de l'asthme.
zhay duh lahs-m.

Toiletries

I need to buy ...
J'ai besoin d'acheter ... / Je dois acheter ...
zhay be-zwahn dahsh-tay ... / zhuh dwah ah-shuh-tay ...

Band-Aids.
les pansements.
lay pahn-suh-mahn.

sunscreen.
de la crème solaire.
duh lah krem so-lair.

toothpaste.
du dentifrice.
dew dahn-tee-freece.

a toothbrush.
une brosse à dents.
ewn bross ah dahn.

a razor.
un rasoir.
uhn rah-zwahr.

shaving cream.
de la crème à raser.
duh lah krem ah rah-zay.

makeup.
du maquillage.
dew mah-kee-yahzh.

tampons.
des tampax.
day tahm-pahks.

a hairbrush.
une brosse.
ewn bross.

new glasses.
des nouvelles lunettes.
day noo-vel lew-net.

new contact lenses.
des nouvelles lentilles de contact.
day noo-vel lahn-teey duh kon-tahkt.

contact lens solution.
de la solution pour lentilles de contact.
duh lah so-lew-syon poor lahn-teey duh kon-tahkt.

Emergencies

Help!
Au secours ! / À l'aide!
oh skoor! / ah led!

Go away!
Va t'en!
vah tahn!

Leave me alone!
Laisse-moi tranquille!
less mwah tahn-keel!

Thief!
Voleur!
vo-luhr!

It's an emergency.
C'est une urgence.
seh-tewn ewr-zhahns.

Call the police!
Appelez la police!
ahp-lay lah po-leece!

Call an ambulance!
Appelez le SAMU!
ahp-play luh sah-mew!

Call a doctor!
Appelez un médecin!
ahp-play uhn made-san!

I need help.
J'ai besoin d'aide.
zhay be-zwahn ded.

I'm lost.
Je suis perdu.
zhuh swee pair-dew.

Crime

I was mugged.
J'étais agressé.
zhay-teh ah-gress-say.

I was assaulted.
J'étais agressé.
zhay-teh ah-gress-say.

I lost ... / Someone stole ...
J'ai perdu ... / Quelqu'un a volé ...
zhay pair-dew ... / kel-kuhn ah vo-lay ...

> **my passport.**
> mon passeport.
> *mon pahs-por.*

my wallet.
mon portefeuille.
mon por-tuh-foy.

my purse.
mon sac à main.
mon sahk ah man.

my camera.
mon appareil-photo.
mon ah-pah-rey-fo-to.

my cell phone.
mon téléphone portable.
mon tay-lay-fon por-tahbl.

my laptop.
mon ordinateur portable.
mon or-dee-nah-tur port-tahbl.

my glasses.
mes lunettes.
meh lew-net.

my luggage.
mes bagagges.
meh bah-gazh.

my backpack.
mon sac à dos.
mon sahk ah doh.

my tour group.
mon groupe.
mon groop.

my mind.
ma tête.
mah tet.

my virginity.
ma virginité.
mah veer-zhee-nee-tay.

Grammar in Five Minutes

Pronouns

Here are some of the most important words you'll need for French: the **personal pronouns.**

SINGULAR		PLURAL	
I	je	**we**	nous
you (informal)	tu	**you** (informal)	vous
you (formal)	vous	**you** (formal)	vous
he	il	**they** (all men/mixed group)	ils
she	elle	**they** (all women)	elles

Politeness and Formality

French speakers distinguish between **formal and informal forms of "you"** when addressing different people. To be on the safe side, use tu only when speaking with close friends or with children. Use vous when addressing anyone else, especially if they're older than you.

Gender

One thing about French that always throws English speakers for a loop: **all French nouns have a gender.** Often, there's no logic behind this system: what makes a book (un livre) a "he" and a door (une porte) a "she" is anyone's guess.

Not only are nouns gendered, but any **adjectives** that describe nouns are gendered as well. An open book is un livre ouvert, but an open door is une porte ouverte. You'll still get your point across even if you make mistakes with this, so don't worry about it too much.

Adjectives After Nouns

As you saw with un livre ouvert, **adjectives in French come after the noun.** This is the opposite of English—we say "the open book," not "the book open." Although there are a few oddball adjectives in French that often come before the noun, this noun-then-adjective rule is nearly universal.

Five Essential Verbs in the Present Tense

All French verbs are **conjugated**—modified slightly in form to reflect who's performing the action of the verb. English verbs are conjugated too—the verb "to be" changes to "I am," "you are," "he is," etc.—but our system is much less complex. Here are five essential French verbs, conjugated fully in the present tense. If you can memorize these, you'll be at a huge advantage.

to be – être

SINGULAR		PLURAL	
je	suis	nous	sommes
tu	es	vous	êtes
il/elle	est	ils/elles	sont

to have – avoir

j'	ai	nous	avons
tu	as	vous	avez
il/elle	a	ils/elles	ont

to do, to make – faire

je	fais	nous	faisons
tu	fais	vous	faites
il/elle	fait	ils/elles	font

to want – vouloir

je	veux	nous	venons
tu	veux	vous	voulez
il/elle	veut	ils/elles	veulent

to go – aller

je	vais	nous	allons
tu	vas	vous	allez
il/elle	va	ils/elles	vont

Acknowledgments

Special thanks to Nancy Johnston, our writer, as well as Anna Medvedovsky, who provided pronunciations and an invaluable fact-checking eye.

Super special thanks to our illustrator, Frank Webster, who took time out from traveling the globe in his private dirigible, *The Princess Calliope*, to supply the wonderful illustrations on the cover and throughout this book.